Praise for
Generation NeXt Marriage

"Where do Gen Xers find the priceless principles to make a marriage work? Most didn't get them in the homes they grew up in, and they didn't get them from the TV or movies they watched or music lyrics they listened to. But Tricia Goyer, an Xer herself, offers real help and real hope for the Gen X marriage and insightful truths for all who work or minister to those in the Gen X age group."

—PAM FARREL, best-selling author of *Men Are Like Waffles—
Women Are Like Spaghetti, Red-Hot Monogamy,*
and *The First Five Years*

"*Generation NeXt Marriage* is a much-needed marriage manual for a generation ready to make the most of marriage. Thoughtful, interactive, well researched, and exceptionally relevant for couples who want to thrive in their marriages, this book is a must for beginning and continuing young couples."

—ELISA MORGAN, CEO, MOPS International and publisher,
FullFill magazine

"Tricia Goyer refuses to play the 'blame game.' This extraordinary Gen Xer, raised in a blended family, steps up to the plate and speaks to ALL generations…but especially to her own. She is gifted and blunt. She shares that it's time to *really LIVE and LOVE YOUR HUSBAND GOD'S WAY*…and tells the reader just how to do that. Tricia is young enough to be my daughter and wise enough to be my mentor. This book is GenXcellent!"

—NANCY COBB, author of *How to Get Your Husband
to Listen to You*

"You'll fall in love with your spouse and Tricia Goyer in this powerful and well-researched expose on marriage. Goyer goes deep, sharing intimate issues of her own love story as well as interviews with fellow Gen Xers and excerpts from the best of

Christian marriage authors. She tops it off with a thought-provoking Bible study sure to help any marriage."

—ELAINE W. MILLER, author of *Splashes of Serenity: Bathtime Reflections for Drained Wives* and *Splashes of Serenity: Bathtime Reflections for Drained Moms*

"*Generation NeXt Marriage* is a transparent, authentic look at modern marriage for Gen Xers. Author Tricia Goyer is warm and friendly, offering teaching without preaching as she shares her own struggles and lessons she's learned the hard way. The book is a fun read for those born in the '60s, '70s, and early '80s as it contains many references to songs, movies, and books they will remember and relate to. I will be recommending this book to many couples!"

—NANCY C. ANDERSON, author of *Avoiding the Greener Grass Syndrome* and regular marriage columnist for Crosswalk.com and CBN.com

"With fascinating facts, eye-opening honesty, and humor in all the right places, Tricia Goyer delivers biblically based advice to Gen Xers on how to negotiate the speed bumps inevitable in marriage—from unrealistic expectations to intimacy to children to communication to money matters. Not a Gen Xer? No problem. *Generation NeXt Marriage* has plenty of timeless truths and advice to go around."

—TAMARA LEIGH, author of *Splitting Harriet* and *Perfecting Kate*

"Tricia Goyer is a strong, godly voice for this generation. Her book *Generation NeXt Marriage* 'gets it.' It is insightful, not to mention fun. A great book for any Gen Xer who is married or is planning to get married."

—RENE GUTTERIDGE, author of the Boo and Occupational Hazards series

GENERATION
NEXT
Marriage

GENERATION
NEXT
Marriage A

TRICIA GOYER

MULTNOMAH
BOOKS

GENERATION NEXT MARRIAGE
PUBLISHED BY MULTNOMAH BOOKS
12265 Oracle Boulevard, Suite 200
Colorado Springs, Colorado 80921
A division of Random House Inc.

All Scripture quotations, unless otherwise indicated, are taken from the Holy Bible, New International Version®. NIV®. Copyright © 1973, 1978, 1984 by International Bible Society. Used by permission of Zondervan Publishing House. All rights reserved. Scripture quotations marked (NASB) are taken from the New American Standard Bible®. © Copyright The Lockman Foundation 1960, 1962, 1963, 1968, 1971, 1972, 1973, 1975, 1977. Used by permission. (www.Lockman.org). Scripture quotations marked (NLT) are taken from the Holy Bible, New Living Translation, copyright © 1996. Used by permission of Tyndale House Publishers Inc., Wheaton, Illinois 60189. All rights reserved. Scripture quotations marked (NKJV) are taken from the New King James Version®. Copyright © 1982 by Thomas Nelson Inc. Used by permission. All rights reserved. Scripture quotations marked (AMP) are taken from The Amplified® Bible. Copyright © 1954, 1958, 1962, 1964, 1965, 1987 by The Lockman Foundation. Used by permission. (www.Lockman.org). Scripture quotations marked (NIrV) are taken from the Holy Bible, New International Reader's Version. Copyright © 1996, 1998 by International Bible Society. All rights reserved throughout the world. Used by permission of International Bible Society. Scripture quotations marked (MSG) are taken from The Message by Eugene H. Peterson. Copyright © 1993, 1994, 1995, 1996, 2000, 2001, 2002. Used by permission of NavPress Publishing Group. All rights reserved. Scripture quotations marked (NLV) are taken from the Holy Bible, New Life Version. Copyright 1969, 1976, 1978, 1983, 1986, 1992, 1997, Christian Literature International, P. O. Box 777, Canby, OR 97013. Used by permission.

In the story about Steven in chapter 5, Steven's name was changed.

ISBN 978-1-59052-910-2

Copyright © 2008 by Tricia Goyer

Published in association with the Books & Such Literary Agency, Janet Kobobel Grant, 52 Mission Circle, Suite 122, PMB 170, Santa Rosa, CA 95409-5370. www.booksandsuch.biz.

MULTNOMAH is a trademark of Multnomah Books, and is registered in the U.S. Patent and Trademark Office. The colophon is a trademark of Multnomah Books.

Library of Congress Cataloging-in-Publication Data
Goyer, Tricia.
   Generation neXt marriage / Tricia Goyer.—1st ed.
     p. cm.
  Includes bibliographical references and index.
   ISBN 978-1-59052-910-2 (alk. paper)
  1. Marriage—Religious aspects—Christianity. 2. Generation X. I. Title.
   BV835.G69 2008
   248.8'44—dc22

                         2007029499

Printed in the United States of America
2008—First Edition

10 9 8 7 6 5 4 3 2 1

To John,
you are forever loved.

My lover is mine and I am his.
Song of Songs 2:16

Love is patient and kind. Love is not jealous or boastful or proud or rude. Love does not demand its own way. Love is not irritable, and it keeps no record of when it has been wronged. It is never glad about injustice but rejoices whenever the truth wins out. Love never gives up, never loses faith, is always hopeful, and endures through every circumstance.

1 CORINTHIANS 13:4–7, NLT

Contents

WHITE WEDDING

It's a nice day for a white wedding.

BILLY IDOL, BILLY IDOL, 1982, CHRYSALIS RECORDS

I was in the sixth grade in 1983 when Billy Idol's song "White Wedding" hit the charts. I remember doodling designs for my wedding dress on the cover of my English book. Funny thing though: Somehow, I forgot to daydream about what would happen *after* I married my Prince Charming. I forgot that a marriage follows the wedding.

Growing up during the 1970s and '80s, I remember hearing Billy Idol's wedding song and, oh, about 2,573 other songs about love. "Addicted to Love" by Robert Palmer, "Crazy Little Thing Called Love" by Queen, "Groovy Kind of Love" by Phil Collins…to name just a few. Yet I can't think of a single romantic song that addressed the day-in, day-out of marriage. Or commitment. Or forever "I do."

Now that's messed up.

Not too surprisingly, I wasn't thinking about forever commitments when I became sexually active in high school. Or when I dumped "loser" boyfriends and exchanged them for better models. Or when I broke many hearts and found mine broken as well.

In fact, I didn't think much about marriage until after I was married in 1989, at age eighteen. I'd signed up for the "I do" after finding someone "safe." Someone who loved me and my son. Someone who had a relationship with the God I was just starting to know.

I fell in love with my new beau, John. And he was great! I had a grand time planning the wedding… And then I woke up one day with this guy sleeping beside me and *What now?* going through my head.

As someone raised by a mom and stepdad who were already contemplating divorce on my wedding day, I couldn't think ahead to what the next year held for John and me, let alone the next fifty years. I wanted the best marriage possible, but I had no idea how to make that happen.

That, my friends, is an anxiety-filled, confusing place to live.

The Scoop on This Book

You may wonder how this book differs from other marriage books out there. For one, I'm not the head of any marriage organization, nor do I have a national radio broadcast. I don't have a degree in psychology or training in marriage enrichment. I'm just a Gen Xer who's written a lot about parenting, life, and marriage over the last ten years. But perhaps my best credential is the fact that John and I have been married for seventeen years. Quite a statement for a thirty-five-year-old!

Although many of our friends' marriages have ended in divorce, John and I are still together. We support each other's careers. We're raising a God-loving family. We volunteer in our church as a team. And most important, we're more in love now than the day we got married.

But if I were to gush about how we've "done everything right," I'd be lying. And you most likely wouldn't want to read another word. After all, Gen Xers have a hard time relating to perfection. Maybe it's because we're *so* very far from it. And we know deep down that everyone else is too.

To be truthful, the last seventeen years haven't been all cupcakes and sprinkles. To put it bluntly, John and I were young and dumb when we got married (or at least I was). And we've made a lot of mistakes (mostly me). But we made a commitment to see this thing through. To work *for* our marriage. To love the other person even when he or she seems unlovely.

We've dealt with many of the same struggles as other young couples, including but not limited to:

❀   communication problems
❀   money woes
❀   emotional burdens from past relationships
❀   struggles with in-laws and out-laws
❀   the joys and anxiety of raising kids
❀   even my draw toward an ex-boyfriend

Without a doubt, this is the hardest book I've ever written. My novels are stories I create in my head; they contain make-believe characters who make plenty of mistakes. The children's and devotional books I write are just plain fun. Even *Generation NeXt Parenting* felt like a breeze compared to writing about my glaring relationship faults. Sure, I shared my struggles with parenting in that book, but now it's time to share my *secrets*. Yikes!

I noticed something else while writing this book. Most of the topics in *Generation NeXt Parenting* are ones you can talk about with any other parent you meet at McDonald's, but this book goes deep and delves into intimate topics—things you share in confidence with your small group or a dear friend…*maybe*.

What This Book Is About…

In this book, you won't find me talking about how to "fix" your spouse or your marriage. Instead, I'm going to talk about our generation, married and grown up—our strengths, our weaknesses, our similarities, and our desire to succeed where so many of our parents and role models failed. I'm also going to dig into God's Word to find hope and help. The idea emerged after I noticed how different my marriage is from those of previous generations. Different doesn't mean wrong…it just means *different*.

Personally, I find myself wanting to do it all—love my spouse, discover God's purpose for my life, make a difference in my community, build a career, and provide my children with every opportunity. *But is that possible while still achieving a semblance of balance?* Each of us needs encouragement and help when dealing with the most complex relationship we'll ever commit to in our lifetime.

Neil Clark Warren—a writer who knows his stuff—issued a challenge in his book *The Triumphant Marriage:* that each year we commit to making our marriages 10 percent better.[1] I like that. Hey, who knows? Maybe you'll even get to 11 percent with the help of this book!

My Take on It

Today's society views marriage as a contract or a legal arrangement. The marriage covenant has been all but eliminated in the world's eyes. To me, that makes marriage the last line of defense for our Christian faith in this secular world. It convicts me to make my marriage the absolute best it can be and to show other couples what a great marriage looks like so they'll want it too.

—Chris, born in 1974

Florida, married thirteen years

Sometimes I think Gen Xers have had more realistic expectations than other generations when it comes to marriage. Seems like my parents' generation had high expectations, and many of them got out when reality set in. I have a lot of hope for my generation. I believe our low divorce rate will stay low. We are fighters, and we don't need things to be perfect. Most of our relationships have not lived up to our expectations (boyfriends, girlfriends, parents, etc.). When our marriage relationships don't live up to our expectations, I don't think we'll be too shocked.

—Jennifer, born in 1969

Wisconsin, married thirteen years

THE FACTS

HOW THE GENERATIONS BREAK DOWN

GI: Born 1900s to 1920s

Silent: Born 1920s to 1940s

Boomer: Born 1940s to 1960s

Xer: Born 1960s to 1980s

Millennial: Born 1980s to 2000s[2]

THE FACTS ABOUT GEN XERS

⚡ Gen Xers consist of 41 million Americans born between 1961 and 1981, plus the 3 million more in that age group who have immigrated here.

⚡ Gen Xers are serious about life. We don't take life as it comes, but give great consideration to critical decisions about our present and future. When it comes to marriage, we want to do it right. We take marriage seriously because half of us were raised in homes where our parents divorced.

⚡ Gen Xers are stressed out. We want to do it all...now. And when we do, we find ourselves overwhelmed—work, family, and the techno-stress that 24/7 communication such as cell phones, e-mail, and instant messaging has brought about. We've bought into following our dreams and finding our purpose. Yet we struggle to balance our spouse, kids, ministry, work, and service.

⚡ Gen Xers love to volunteer, to give, to help, to make a difference! In fact, a recent study revealed that out of different age groups who volunteer regularly, the percentage of Gen Xers was higher than any other (31.2 percent). And that doesn't even account for those who volunteer on more than one committee.

⚡ Gen Xers are self-reliant, yet highly spiritual. We're skeptical, yet eager to apply what we *do* believe to our everyday lives. We're realistic, not idealistic. Our faith has to be truly lived out or we won't buy into it.

⚡ According to a recent George Barna study, only 28 percent of Gen Xers (ages 20–37) attend church, compared to 51 percent of Builders (58+). Yet a *Newsweek* article recently suggested that "81 percent of Gen X mothers and 78 percent of fathers say they plan eventually to send their young child to Sunday school or some other kind of religious training."

Gen X: The Married Life... Who Would've Thought?

The facts are in. The generation that once bore labels such as "slacker" and "grunge" has gone G-rated. Once Gen Xers get serious about life, *family* now means the most to us. Marriage matters. And we want not just an okay marriage, but one filled with love, commitment, and care.

Yet as Gen Xers, we—more than any other generation—also have a hard time understanding just how to accomplish that. Divorce skyrocketed in our nation during our formative years, doubling the rate of the prior generation.

Growing up, we set a new standard for sexual activity as teens, and we bore more kids out of wedlock. (I confess to both.) And some of us have already experienced one or more divorces.

"Statistics show that of every ten marriages in America today, five end in divorce and three have partners dissatisfied with marriage," write Patrick and Connie Lawrence in *How to Build a More Intimate Marriage*. "Only two out of ten couples express satisfaction with the marriage."[3]

Yet there is hope. Hope found in the Word of God. Hope that God is aware of the obstacles we face. And faith that He *can* help us, even in our marriages. And boy, am I clinging to that word *hope*.

I write this as someone who has made a lot of mistakes. Some of my biggest struggles have been in my marriage. These are not easy mistakes to confess, but I will share them for two reasons:

1. Because by sharing my mistakes, I also can share the *triumph* found in God alone.
2. Because to Gen Xers, relationships and authenticity mean a lot. We won't give two seconds of our time to a phony. We crave the real deal.

In addition to my story, this book also offers comments from other Gen Xers. Like me, they're willing to "share all." Some give their names; others chose not to in order to protect their families. Regardless, I know that their words will touch you just the same.

As one Gen Xer said when answering my interview questions: "This is soul-baring stuff." I agree. But in the end, I pray it will be worth it. *Because only when our souls are stirred can our lives be transformed.*

Throughout this book, God's Word will be used as home base for strengthening marriage. The stories of fellow Gen Xers will be the real-life examples that hit Truth out of the park.

And while I don't claim that every marriage issue will be covered within these pages, you can see from the chapter titles that we'll touch on the biggies. It's my goal to help you and the person you love most in this world (or should love most) take a look at some of those important issues in your married life, view them in light of today's world, and then process them through Scripture.

As Billy Idol sang, "It's a nice day for a white wedding. It's a nice day to start again."

My Take on It

I think that in society today, the idea of marriage is no longer a sacred thing, and that makes me very angry! People look at marriage like, "Oh well, if it doesn't work this time, we just get divorced and try with someone else." People need instant gratification these days and no one wants to work hard, so we have high divorce rates and broken homes. I made mistakes when I was younger, but now that my marriage was given a second chance, I look at the way things are and it makes me sick! It makes me want to work harder and defy the odds by being married to my soul mate until we die and to raise our children in a happy home with both of their parents.

—Dee, born in 1975

Michigan, married ten years

I think that people give up on marriage too easily. It's not something to be entered into lightly, yet people do it all the time. I think this affects my own marriage by giving both my husband and me more determination to make it—conforming is a bad thing! We've discussed the failed marriages around us and tried to analyze them along with our own marriage—helping to keep our faith strong in ourselves.

—Amy, born in 1971

South Carolina, married five years

MORE FACTS

1. **Gen Xers desire to maintain the nuclear family.** On Wikipedia, the term Gen X marriage is defined like this: Gen X quietly practices their tolerance, as shown by the increase in interracial marriages and adoptions, experimenting with alternative lifestyles such as living together before marriage, while not yet showing a desire to impose their personal individual choices on society via legalisms. Gen Xers moving into marriage and parenting are expressing a stronger desire to maintain the nuclear family. Some Gen Xers delayed marriage in order to more carefully choose/find a mate for a lifetime. If the marriage does end in divorce, both parents stay involved with the children via joint custody.[4]

2. **Gen Xers know the facts.** The percentage of new marriages predicted to end in divorce or separation over a lifetime is as follows:

   - 1960: 33%
   - 2000: 50%[5]

3. ***Gen Xers want a soul mate.*** The Whitehead-Popenoe study found: America's twenty-somethings are looking for a lifetime soul mate. An overwhelming majority (94 percent) of never-married singles agree that the search for an emotional and spiritual "soul mate" is the first consideration in marriage. There is no significant gender gap in the response. Eighty-eight percent of never-married singles in the 20–29 age range are optimistic that such a soul mate exists and that, when the time is right, they will find that special someone. Seventy-eight percent agree that a couple should not get married unless they are prepared to stay together for life.[6]

4. ***Gen Xers' uncertainty started in the home.*** "When the bottom fell out of the institution of marriage, Xers were the victims. And it left a scar. The divorce rate and the percentage of children born outside of marriage in the United States doubled between 1965 and 1977. In the 1970s, their Boomer parents achieved the dubious distinction of having the world's highest divorce rate—40 percent of all marriages ended in divorce. A 1995 *American Demographics* article reported that 'more than 40 percent of today's young adults spent at least some time in a single-parent family by age 16.'"[7]

5. ***Gen Xers long to be accepted.*** Experts claim that the strongest desire of Gen Xers, due to the loneliness and alienation of their splintered family attachments, is acceptance and belonging. *Unfortunately, we often get married only to discover that our needs still go unmet.*

6. ***Gen Xers believe in family values.*** We want to have a good marriage that will last "until death do us part." Yet we question if we're doing it right. We wonder if our marriage, too, will be absorbed in a disheartening statistic. To do it right, we must discover a better way.

Why Hope? Why Try?

For our happiness. Married people are more than twice as likely to be happy as divorced or never-married individuals.[8]

For our lives. Married families have higher incomes. The economic benefits of marriage are not limited to the middle class; some 70 percent of never-married mothers could escape poverty if they were married to the father of their children.[9]

For our kids. Children from intact families are less likely to be depressed, to have difficulty in school, to have behavior problems, or to use marijuana.[10] *(The older I get, the more I realize what I missed as a child. Namely, growing up with two parents who loved each other unconditionally and modeled a happy and healthy marriage.)*

For our core values. One 2000 study conducted by the Radcliffe Public Policy Center found that the job characteristic most often ranked as "very important" by men between the ages of twenty-one and thirty-nine was "having a work schedule that allows me to spend time with my family." At a time when people are asked to work longer hours, that same study found that some 70 percent of these men wanted to spend more time with their families and were willing to sacrifice pay to do so.[11]

For our God. More than all the reasons above, we want our marriages to succeed for the love of God. He has placed us in this time in history for a reason, and as Gen Xers we long to succeed for His glory!

My Take on It

I see marriage as a proving ground, a place where I'm most challenged and changed. I think society says that too—that marriage is tough. The difference is that I'm in this relationship until the Lord calls me home, whereas society says divorce is an option. That knowledge makes it difficult to stay when things get hard. But the reminder that I'm not alone in this, that there is a greater plan at work and a very good God at the center, makes it worth walking through the fire and holding fast to the truth.

—Amy, born in 1970

Georgia, married eleven years

I'm fighting even harder to make sure the hedges of protection are around my household. I'm doing all I can to keep my end of the vows so there is no opportunity for the enemy to kill and steal and destroy. I'm staying on my knees for my marriage and family. I'm holding on to *who* God is and what He's promised in order to find my way in this life. He's taking me step by step through the minefield, and He's never led me astray.

—Allison, born in 1974

Florida, married thirteen years

Final note: One more thing I want to mention is the use of song lyrics from the 1970s and '80s in the text. Do I quote these singers and groups because they're upstanding people who have answers? Not at all. I quote them because their music defined our times. I quote them not because they have the answers, but because they reveal our questions. Within their lyrics lie the thoughts, longings, hopes, and confusion of an entire generation. And within God's holy Word are the answers we sought then and still seek now.

And One More Thing...

"This was the generation, after all, for which the term 'latchkey kid' was coined. The end result was that Gen X put off marriage and having children in record numbers. Gen X helped push the average age of first marriage over 27 for men and 25 for women. In 1970, the median age at first marriage was 22.5 years for men, and 20.6 years for women. So far, the divorce rate for Gen X stands at an unusually low 8 percent, but if history is a guide, most would agree it's too early in the marriage cycle of the group to get a proper read on its potential outcome."[12]

1

YOU Might THINK

Dealing with Unrealistic Expectations in the Reality of Marriage

I'm crazy, but all I want is you.

THE CARS, HEARTBEAT CITY, 1984, ELEKTRA RECORDS

Before we got married, John and I spent hours and hours talking. We discussed our growing-up years, our hopes and dreams, our likes and dislikes. We literally spent every free moment together. I thought I knew him pretty well. After four months of dating we were engaged, and we married five months later.

I'd found the man for me. For life.

Even though I didn't realize it at the time, I had expectations of what life would be like after we were married. Very unrealistic expectations, I soon discovered. For example, I'd visited John's apartment on many occasions, and I could tell he was a neat freak. His bed was always made. The dishes were washed and put away. He did his own laundry and ironed his own clothes. What a guy!

I was just the opposite. In fact, one thing my mother repeatedly told me when I was growing up was, "I'd hate to see what *your* house will be like when I'm not around to pick up after you."

Cool, I thought. *John will do all the housecleaning…this will work out perfectly.*

Okay, let's stop right here. I'll wait while you finish laughing.

You see, John had his own expectations.

Great, John thought. *Once we get married Trish will be around, so I won't have to do all the housecleaning.*

As you can imagine, we both had unrealistic expectations. And we were both hugely disappointed!

Now, if those had been the only expectations we had for each other, then married life would have been fairly manageable. But they weren't. In fact, our expectations were just one drop in the tidal wave. Our differing thoughts on issues like money, child-rearing, sex, and our extended families soon created waves, as deep-seated emotions, past experiences, and firm opinions stirred the sandy beaches of our honeymoon paradise.

Ohmigosh! Who is this person I married? I wondered, my chin set and my arms firmly crossed over my chest. *When did he get so opinionated and stubborn?*

Crazy for You

It's all brand-new.

MADONNA, THE IMMACULATE COLLECTION, 1990, SIRE RECORDS

Growing up, all of us develop expectations of what marriage is like. And when we finally meet that special someone, our expectations reach an all-time high. *This is going to be GREAT!* we think as we confess our love to each other. *This is the person I've looked for all my life!*

And in the beginning, things *are* great. Discussions focus on happy topics like lifelong dreams and values and our future children. It never crosses our mind to talk about real-life stuff. In fact, I like to compare the dating relationship to M&M's candies. We're so excited about the shiny, varied colors of our attraction and the sweet chocolate of romance that we don't pay much attention to the other person's nutty opinions, habits, and real-ness…until we bite in.

I didn't realize until after saying "I do" that marriage isn't about *the future*. It's about the present. It's not about future careers or imaginary children. It's about everyday stuff, like toothpaste tubes and laundry piles, or *Monday Night Football* and karate films versus chick flicks.

As women, we picture our future spouse as the man who will continue to listen and care, continue to flatter us and attend to our whims. And the man in our lives really *does* think we'll continue to shoot hoops together in the driveway…or sit next to him and hand over tools as he works on his car. After all, this is what life was like with each other before the wedding. Why would we expect any different?

Willard F. Harley Jr., author of *His Needs, Her Needs*, writes:

> It is not uncommon for women, when they are single, to join men in pursuing their interests. They find themselves hunting, fishing, playing football, and watching movies they would never have chosen on their own. After marriage wives often try to interest their husbands in activities more to their own liking. If their attempts fail, they may encourage their husbands to continue their recreational activities without them.[1]

The biggest unrealistic expectation is the notion that things will "continue like they did when we dated" (with the bonus of living together and the added fun of sex, of course!).

What newlyweds often forget is that dating is more about impressing the other person than revealing our true selves. Sure, I hiked with my beau…because I wanted to *spend time with him*. I also made sure I looked my best. I sacrificed time and money for "just perfect" hair and stylish clothes. I exercised and sacrificed ice cream *and* cookies to stay in shape and look like the type of person John would be proud to have on his arm.

And yes, John tromped through the mall with me for hours at a time and wore the new clothes I picked out for him. After all, he was just like one of those birds that display its brightly colored feathers, strutting its stuff, as part of its mating ritual. John was on his best behavior.

As Madonna sang, "It's all brand-new...I'm crazy for you." But oftentimes we discover that the things that make us crazy-in-love are the very things that drive us insane during marriage. Can anyone give me an amen?

My Take on It

I didn't have a clue what it would be like. I was eighteen, a sophomore in college, working two jobs. We were planning to wait until after college to get married, but our plans were moved up three years when my wife-to-be got pregnant. For me, it was the time to step up and take responsibility. Expectations were simply that we would survive and I would finish my degree. I thank God both goals were accomplished, due in no small part to my wife's support and equal dedication to our family.

—Chris, born in 1974

Florida, married thirteen years

I must have had some big expectations, because the very next morning my husband and I got in our first fight *ever*, and I was like, "Huh? What happened here? What have I done? Oh, noooooo!" I had no clue what I was getting into. I was just pregnant and didn't want my baby to be illegitimate, and I was getting pressure. Oh sure, I had planned my wedding and wanted a white dress and all that fun stuff, but I never really gave marriage any consideration. Sorta like how I wanted a baby but I never considered parenting... Clueless.

—Katie, born in 1972

Montana, married seven years

How Soon Is Now?

How can you say, I go about things the wrong way...

THE SMITHS, HATFUL OF HOLLOW, 1984, ROUGH TRADE

The problem, of course, isn't only that marriage is vastly different from what we imagined. The problem also arises from our efforts to transform our expectations into reality.

I'm sure all of us can think of things we wanted to change about our new husband or wife when we first got married. *Maybe there are things you're still working on!*

But the truth is that changing the other person doesn't work, mainly because it's not our job. This quote says it well: "Part of being a good spouse is to help keep your home in order, putting everything in its place. However, it is not your duty to put your spouse in his or her place."[2] *Ouch.*

I can feel my cheeks reddening with this one, because boy did I try! And that went about as far as my minivan on E: nowhere. The reason, I discovered, is that when we try to force our spouses to live up to our expectations, one thing is missing: honor.

Honor for our spouse.

Honor for God the Creator.

Now, *honor* isn't a word we think about much this day and age, but when I looked it up, the definition was simple:

     a. to hold in respect; esteem.

     b. to show respect for.

When we have expectations of our spouse and secretly wish for him or her to change, discontentment slides in, booting out respect. The thumbs-up we offered during the dating years turns into a thumbs-down.

But since we don't want to out-and-out complain, we show our disapproval in subtle ways—by making little comments, sending disapproving glances, or posting sticky notes inscribed with Scripture verses to the remote control: "I will set before my eyes *no vile thing*," (Psalm 101:3, emphasis mine). As if the other person isn't smart enough to know what we're doing!

Our actions are justified, or so we think. After all, we have a lot riding on this other person.

"Marriage is to human relations what monotheism is to theology. It is a decision to put all the eggs in one basket, to go for broke, to bet all of the marbles," writes Mike Mason in *The Mystery of Marriage*.

Is there any abandonment more pure, more supreme, more radically self-abnegating than that of putting one's entire faith in just one God, the Lord of all, in such a way as to allow that faith to have a searching impact on every corner of one's entire life? On the level of human relations, there is only one act of trust which can begin to approach this one, and that is the decision to believe in one other person, and to believe so robustly as to be ready to squander one's whole life on that one.[3]

Yet to truly believe in one other person…we need to *believe in* Him. To trust that God knows his or her strengths and weaknesses even better than we do. God also knows our expectations (no matter how unrealistic they are).

The truth is, these are things God uses as the months and years progress. Issues, conflicts, and struggles can draw us closer to Him if we remember to bring our expectations to God in prayer. They are also the things that will show us what loving imperfect people is all about.

"Yes," you say, "but I still have to live with her! Should I just throw my hands up and stuff my expectations like cheeks full of sugary marshmallows, pretending these things don't matter?"

No, but here's what you can do:

1. Understand that expectations can hurt your relationship.

   " 'And they lived happily ever after' is one of the most tragic sentences in literature," author Joshua Lievman once wrote. "It's tragic because it's a falsehood. It is a myth that has led generations to expect something from marriage that is not possible."

(Sure, Cinderella got Prince Charming, but we didn't get to see the rest of the story. Just how did she handle it when he continued to forget to put down the toilet seat?)

"The enemy is an expert archer with lots of practice aiming fiery darts," adds Beth Moore. "When women are the targets, often the bull's-eye is childhood dreams or expectations. We grew up believing in Cinderella, yet some of us feel as if our palace turned out to be a duplex, our prince turned out to be a frog, and the wicked stepmother turned out to be our mother-in-law. Our fairy godmother apparently lost our addresses."[4]

2. **Look in the mirror first.**

"Success in marriage is more than finding the right person; it is being the right person," wrote the poet Robert Browning. To me, being the right person is looking at myself through my spouse's eyes. It's seeing the things I do that irritate him and working to fix those things that have merit (such as forgetting to do the errands he's repeatedly asked me to do). It's asking God to reveal areas of much-needed transformation in our own hearts.

"'Managing self' means to do what I can do with *me* when I can't do anything about the circumstances surrounding me," writes Cindi Wood, author of *The Frazzled Female*.[5]

A lot can happen in my marriage, and my spouse can come up short on many counts, but I can work on myself. I can bring my heart, motives, and actions before God and ask Him to change *me*.

3. **Love your spouse...anyway.**

According to the *Life Application Bible Commentary* on John 15:17:

"Our world wants love to be spontaneous and driven by feeling. But Jesus knows our deeper need. We know we ought to love even when we don't feel like it because we want others to love us when we are unlovable. In Jesus we find both the supreme model for loving and the supreme resource. He commands us to love, and he helps us accomplish his command.

"Jesus knew that if we would practice love, then the feelings of love would follow naturally. If we waited to be motivated by affection for others, we would never love others. Treating others with honor and respect (even when we don't feel they deserve it) may generate good will and affection. If we understand how deeply we are loved by God in spite of our sin, we will be pushed in the direction of loving others ourselves. Those who do not realize God's love for them find it difficult to love others."[6]

An old Greek proverb says, "The heart that loves is always young." No matter how many years you've been married, that impressionable guy you dated is still somewhere in there, wanting to be loved, appreciated, and admired. Remember the things that drew you to him? Yes, well, *love* him for those things. Love with words and actions. Focus on the good.

4. Expect a blessing.

Matthew 5:9 says, "God blesses those who work for peace, for they will be called the children of God" (NLT). Ephesians 6:7–8 says: "Work with enthusiasm, as though you were working for the Lord rather than for people. Remember that the Lord will reward each one of us for the good we do, whether we are slaves or free" (NLT).

I can't tell you the number of times I looked at John and saw something in his life that didn't meet my expectations. Yet when I gave my expectations to God, worked on myself, and loved John just as he was, a wonderful thing happened. God worked on *John's* heart in ways I'd never dreamed. And amazingly, God found a way to do it without my nagging and prodding!

"How soon is now?" sang the Smiths. Start today.

MY TAKE ON IT

I think unrealistic expectations are the key to so much unhappiness in marriage—placing expectations on our spouse to fill needs that only God can and *should* fill. If we ask our spouses to take that place, then we make them idols and they will fail. As I look back on the early years of our marriage, many of my disappointments came from expecting my husband to do all the changing while I stubbornly insisted that he knew what he was getting when he married me. Even now, I have to be careful that I'm meeting his needs without burdening him with my unrealistic expectations. I wish I had this down pat. I just pray that God will continue to open my eyes and my heart to be the supportive spouse he needs without the strings of expectations that set him up to fail.

—Cara, born in 1974

Indiana, married ten years

AND ONE MORE THING...

"Everywhere else, throughout society, there are fences, walls, burglar alarms, unlisted numbers, the most elaborate precautions for keeping people at a safe distance. But in marriage all of that is reversed. In marriage the walls are down, and not only do the man and woman live under the same roof, but they sleep under the same covers. Their lives are wide open, and as each studies the life of the other and attempts to make some response to it, there are no set procedures to follow, no formalities to stand on. A man and a woman face each other across the breakfast table, and somehow through a haze of crumbs and curlers and mortgage payments they must encounter one another. That is the whole purpose and mandate of marriage. All sorts of other purposes have been dreamed up and millions of excuses invented for avoiding this central and indispensable task. But the fact is that marriage is grounded in nothing else but the pure, wild grappling of soul with soul, no holds barred. There is no rule book for this, no law to invoke except the law of love."[7]

2 History NEVER REPEATS

Revisiting Your Relationship Role Models

...I tell myself before I go to sleep.

SPLIT ENZ, WAIATA, 1981, A&M

History never repeats, I tell myself before I go to sleep," Split Enz sang in 1981. (Do you remember? They were one of the first bands on MTV.) My response? "I sure hope it *doesn't* repeat!"

I, unfortunately, am a typical Gen Xer. My mom has been married three times (and none of those marriages were to my biological dad). And my stepdad, who raised me, has been married twice and lived with various other girlfriends over the years. Even now, in their late fifties, they still aren't in happy places with their current relationships.

I don't know about you, but when I first got married, I wanted to make sure my marriage would be different. I wanted it to be better. *I will not have a marriage like my parents had,* I vowed. *I will commit to my spouse and remember that a marriage takes work. I will stay married for life.*

Even though I didn't want history to repeat itself, I knew that the relationship role models I grew up with had a deep impact on me. In fact, they had a deep impact on our whole generation.

[Gen Xers] grew up in an "anti-child" era as their Boomer (and a few Silent) gen-eration parents focused more on their own personal needs. They quoted Dr. Benjamin Spock, saying that the best gift you could give your child was a happy parent. To achieve this status, you had to focus on doing your own thing....

In America the number of children involved in divorces increased by 300 percent in the forty year period from 1940 to 1980.

The divorce boom meant that many an Xer spent every second weekend at their other parent's home, and saw a profusion of different family relation-ships, such as "dad's girlfriend," "mom's previous ex-husband," "my second step-father," or "my stepsister's half-brother's mother." No wonder Xers are skeptical about relationships, yet feel a need to fill the void with something else.[1]

This describes me perfectly. As an adult I'm still juggling the effects of my par-ents' many relationships.

Maybe you, too, deal with visiting two sets of parents in two separate states, meeting the new stepmom or girlfriend (and praying this one will stick), or feeling fed up with giving a parent marital advice (again).

"Even if you think you don't have any lingering issues, I invite you to discover how the divorce has shaped your life," writes Jen Abbas, author of *Generation Ex.* "You did not experience the fullness of what God designed for you in a family, and so you *have* been hurt. It's just that you are part of a generation that has learned to see these scars as normal."[2]

How about you? Is this your norm?

Maybe you were one of the lucky ones who had a mom and dad that provided a great relational example for you to follow. Even if that's the case, I imagine that divorce has touched your life in some way, shaped your idea of marriage into something different than the one modeled for you.

"Most of us learned little about marriage growing up, even when our parents did stay together," says Pamela Paul in *The Starter Marriage and the Future of Matrimony*. "Their marriages looked very different from what we imagined for ourselves."[3]

But before we dig in to the upcoming chapters and talk about what we want to do differently, let's look back on the relationships that molded our idea of marriage.

My Take on It

I think that Gen Xers often don't know how to make marriage work. We don't have any examples of what marriage should be. If you look at our families, there's generally not a lot of good modeling there. If you look to Hollywood, you're not going to find any positive examples of good marriages. If you look to media, you won't see any news stories about healthy marriages. Instead we have reality dating shows like *The Bachelor,* in which someone proposes after six weeks of dating twenty-five women at once!

—Jessica, born in 1975

Iowa, married four years

My generation grew up with a lot of divorce, and we don't want that in our own marriages. I see couples waiting to marry until much later. Most of our friends married in their late twenties or thirties. And it feels like more and more people are living together first, mainly because they fear divorce and feel they need that assurance that the relationship will work.

—MD, born in 1968

New Jersey, married eleven years

All Those Years Ago

You had control of our smiles and tears, all those years ago.

George Harrison, Living in England, 1981, Dark Horse

As George Harrison sang, many of our smiles and tears are the result of outside influences. And growing up, no one was more influential in our lives than our parents. They were our world. No matter how dysfunctional, or perhaps even how great, they were all we knew. Whether our parents displayed passivity or volatility, that became the norm for what we imagined marriage to be like.

"The first stage of value development takes place from birth to approximately seven years of age," write Dr. Rick and Kathy Hicks in *Boomers, Xers, and Other Strangers*. "Just as a foot leaves its imprint in the sand, the things a young child experiences affect his values. What he sees happening in his family and the world around him is the 'right' way for things to be done. There is no logic or reasoning involved. It is a matter of seeing, absorbing, and accepting."[4]

As we got older, we grew more and more aware that *our* home life wasn't the same as everyone else's. We noted differences and began to form our own values. We made lists of things we liked. We started understanding how other people's actions hurt us, and inwardly we promised ourselves that we would do things differently when we had the chance.

One example of "doing things differently" is the fact that many in our generation wait until later in life to marry. Others choose to live with their boyfriend or girlfriend instead of tying the knot.

According to the US Census Bureau, 49.7 percent of the United States' 111.1 million households were headed by married couples in 2005; this means that for the first time, there was a higher percentage of unmarried couples than married.

When it comes to the age of Gen Xers marrying, I was in the minority—I married at eighteen. Thankfully, I married someone who had better relationship role models than I did. John's parents are still married after forty-four years. They'd be the first to admit that they've had conflict over the years, but they've stuck it out, modeled what a loving relationship looks like, and still care for each other after all this time. It's a great example for us to look to!

Revisiting relationship role models means understanding and accepting how you were affected—sometimes negatively, other times positively.

My Take on It

Well, as bad as it sounds, by having my parents divorced and living two weeks in one life and two weeks in another, I saw what worked and what didn't. My husband was blessed to be raised by a stepdad and a mom who were fairly stable into his early teens [his parents divorced when he was not quite two]. So we both had some idea of what messes up relationships and what makes them stronger.

—Tiff, born in 1976

Michigan, married ten years

My parents showed me that marriage and love are a commitment. You don't walk away. You work hard, play hard, and love hard. They demonstrated that when God's in the center, you can make a marriage work. Thirty-nine years later, they are still together and still working hard to have a great marriage. I want to have that legacy of success.

—Cara, born in 1974

Indiana, married eleven years

My mom has been married and divorced three times, so there really isn't anything positive to say *except* … I learned that divorce really hurts kids, and I could never do that to my own.

—Kristy, born in 1970

Texas, married fifteen years

The Negative

Even if your parents didn't divorce, if you grew up in the 1970s and '80s, divorce likely impacted you in some way. Maybe your parents didn't split up, but a good friend's did. Maybe your boyfriend's parents were divorced. Even children from intact homes were still impacted by the widespread divorce we saw during our growing-up years.

> When children of divorce become adults, they are badly frightened that their relationships will fail, just like the most important relationship in their parents' lives failed. They mature with a keen sense that their growing-up experiences did not prepare them for love, commitment, trust, marriage, or even for the nitty-gritty of handling and resolving conflicts.... Their decisions about whether or not to marry are shadowed by the experience of growing up in a home where their parents could not hold it together. They are no less eager than their peers who grew up in intact families for passionate love, sexual intimacy, and commitment. But they are haunted by powerful ghosts from their childhoods that tell them that they, like their parents, will not succeed.[5]

Fear. A lack of preparation for love, commitment, trust. Haunted by powerful ghosts. It seems like our marriages are destined for failure, right? Wrong.

 ## The Positive

The positive spin for Gen Xers who were affected by divorce is our determination to be different. People called us nonconformists for years; now we're living up to that label.

"Gen X is rebelling against the ultimate rebels by romanticizing marriage and many of the 'traditional' virtues that Boomers (often inadvertently) left behind," writes Pamela Paul.[6]

The Barna Research Group agrees. "Often described as pessimistic, self-centered and brooding, the [Baby Buster] generation is now becoming more family-oriented (more than twice as many Busters are married today as was true just ten years ago, and millions more have children today than a decade earlier), producing a slow but growing acceptance of more traditional Christian activity."[7] (*Baby Busters* is the term the Barna Group uses to describe Gen Xers born between 1965 and 1983.)

Knowing the pain that marital conflict can cause, many Gen Xers work hard to succeed. Personally, I have dozens of marriage books lining my bookshelves, and over the past year John and I have made it a priority to read a chapter out of one of these books every morning before he heads to work. Is this because we have a bad marriage? No! It's rather because we want to make ours great. We are proactive because we have seen the pain caused when marriage isn't given priority in a couple's lives.

The Most Positive of Positives

Of course, the most positive aspect of growing up in a time when many marriages struggled and failed is realizing that where we lack marriage role models, knowledge, or even the desire to give our all to this marriage thing, God fills in the holes. These holes may have been caused by lack of a good foundation, or they may be holes caused by pain from the past. Whatever they are, God can be strong in all these areas in which we are weak.

Remember 2 Corinthians 12:9–10? It's one of my favorite Scriptures.

But he said to me, "My grace is sufficient for you, for my power is made perfect in weakness." Therefore I will boast all the more gladly about my weaknesses, so that Christ's power may rest on me. That is why, for Christ's sake, I delight in weaknesses, in insults, in hardships, in persecutions, in difficulties. For when I am weak, then I am strong.

What a powerful concept for our generation to grasp. In all the ways that we feel weak from a lack of good role models or foundation or dedication, God has a chance to be strong. Yes, we may still be carrying wounds from our youth. But imagine the double witness of facing our marriage challenges with determination.

No doubt about it, humans are a flawed group. We fail to live up to our own lofty expectations every day. Does that mean we should quit trying? Of course not! The athlete doesn't quit practicing in the midst of pain. He keeps at it because the goal of winning offers more satisfaction than any relief from his present discomfort. A mountain climber is not satisfied with *attempting* to climb Mount Everest. The pleasure comes with reaching the summit. No one who's been married will tell you that the union is easy, but any couple who has celebrated a fiftieth anniversary will testify that the sum of the ebb and flow of marital satisfaction is far more fulfilling than the strain of any particular incident. In fact, it's often through the trials, one might argue, that a marriage is strengthened. Few things are more deeply satisfying than accomplishing that which was thought impossible.[8]

When we tackle the mountain of obstacles faced by couples today, wouldn't it be great to say we made it? What a testimony to God's strength in our lives if we are able to overlook our wounds because we are so focused on the victory we achieved through God.

I want to make it to the top of the mountain, despite the struggle it took to get there! I want to be known as one of the faithful, someone who turned the statistics upside down and reversed the tide of divorce. I'd like my example to encourage others—especially my children, whose whole world centers on the commitment their father and I make to each other, with the strength of God.

MY TAKE ON IT

I think the trend now is that people are waiting to get married. They have seen the effect of divorce on children and family (they themselves being affected), and they don't want to go down that road. People are becoming more committed, are willing to work things out rather than just end it and move on. However, a successful marriage is not always the holy union between man/wife/ God that God intended. Sometimes marriages work out not because God has changed hearts and lives, but because Xers, as overachievers, are not going to allow personal failure. They will not be divorced because that is what people who fail do. And besides, what would people say?

—Anne, born 1973

Washington, married twelve years

The trials of marriage are not such a shock anymore. As a child, I used to see divorce as the common resolution to those trials. But our children are now seeing that marriage is worth fighting for. They certainly aren't oblivious to the problems, but they are learning that you can stand and fight rather than turn your back and walk away.

—Michelle, born in 1971

Ohio, married thirteen years

AND ONE MORE THING...

"Opinion surveys show that in the minds of most twenty- and thirty-somethings, marriage ranks higher in importance than career; Gen X considers 'being a good wife/mother or husband/father' to be the most important sign of success—ahead of money, fame, power, religion, and being true to oneself." [9]

In its 1998 report "Time to Repaint the Gen X Portrait," the Yankelovich research firm warns, "Expect Gen Xers to place paramount importance on family togetherness." Clearly Xers want to build their own happy families. They aspire to more children than their predecessors; 63 percent believe that "the good life" means having two or more kids. Over half claim that they get most or all of their satisfaction from home and family, rather than from away-from-home activities like work or friends. Gen X's family ideals remain traditional in several ways. Of those surveyed, 92 percent believed that "it's critical for children today to have activities that anchor them to their families, like regular sit-down family meals or weekly religious services." Eighty-five percent believe "people should pass on to their children a sense of belonging to a particular religion or racial or national tradition," and 83 percent felt that "even though men have changed a lot, women are still the main nurturers. [10]

MY TAKE ON IT

I think Gen Xers *want* to have the lifelong relationship our grandparents and great-grandparents once had but see the realities of life coming in too much. I believe they want the "happily ever after" but may not realize just how tough that is going to be until they are in the trenches. We were raised, those of us who are girls, to believe there's a Prince Charming out there just waiting to sweep us off our feet and make our lives perfect. We were set up for a fall.

—Allison, born in 1974

Florida, married thirteen years

I think most of us Gen Xers have matured by this point in our lives and maybe no longer have such a disposable view of marriage. When I was preparing to get married I remember thinking that if my marriage didn't work out, I could just get a divorce. And I almost did. But Gen Xers, like myself, have been around long enough now to have experienced the pain that our own selfishness causes. Most of us have grown up by now. Our view of marriage is beginning to change. We are more nostalgic, longing for the "good old days," when people were "happy." We want to be whole and have marriages that are genuine. At the same time we are realistic and know that the old days weren't quite so idyllic. This time around we want marriage to work for both spouses. We are looking for a marriage that fulfills our needs and our purpose as individuals and as a couple. We are looking for something real and lasting.

—Anne, born in 1973

Washington, married twelve years

3

TOGETHER Forever

Committed for Life

...and never to part.

RICK ASTLEY, 1987, WHENEVER YOU NEED SOMEBODY, RCA

Two years after Rick Astley (one of my eighties faves) released "Together Forever," John and I got married. It was then that I promised "till death do us part." Of course, those were easy words to say as I stood there in my white dress with ruffled train, the flash of cameras brightening John's smile even more, but living out the ideal has challenged me more than I ever imagined.

I wanted to believe, as Rick Astley sang, that it was "something to last for all time." But as the years went by, I had to move beyond my romantic notions concerning marriage; I had to work hard to make it last. Like anything I really wanted to succeed at, such as getting good grades in college, becoming a published author, or raising godly kids, I had to train myself to be successful.

Jim Burns, the author of *Creating an Intimate Marriage*, compares the work that goes into a healthy marriage as similar to training for a marathon.

If we want to have a healthy relationship, we have to put in the training and do what it takes to make it work. Despite the way Hollywood depicts intimacy, good things don't just "happen"; proper training is vital to accomplishing any goal. Contentment is a result of our proper training! Just like running a marathon, an intimate marriage takes an investment of time, energy, focus, and sometimes the help and coaching of others. It may mean something as simple as setting up daily routines that you know in the long run will produce more intimacy in the relationship. Sure there are sacrifices to make, but the result of intimacy and contentment make the effort worthwhile.[1]

Hard work doesn't sound very romantic, but neither does divorce or splitting assets or sharing kids fifty-fifty. I've been willing to put in the work, and thankfully John has too. I think the same can be said of many Gen Xers.

The result of our childhood experiences has been not, as one might expect, a wariness of matrimony. Instead, today's generation is reacting against divorce by romanticizing marriage—that supposedly problematic institution our predecessors so clearly rejected....

Welcome back, matrimony. Suburbia. Two to three children in the planning. Maternity fashion. Even *housewives*. We long for the marriages that Boomers grew up in and then renounced.... In many ways, Xers are embracing some of these values because they too have lived through uncertain formative years.[2]

Welcome back, matrimony. I like that! In fact, I get weepy every time I read the anniversary announcements in our community newspaper. You know the kind: "Muriel and Melvin James, married sixty years, invite you to join them in their celebration of marriage."

I also love reading romantic stories from the post–World War II era. Stories of men and women who met after the war, got married three weeks later, and still light up when the other person walks in the room—even after all these years.

Today we would think a person was crazy to marry after only knowing someone for three weeks. Personally, I think the difference is not the length of engagement but the depth of commitment. If you talk to these long-married couples, as I have (through interviewing veterans for my World War II novels), you discover that they faced the same situations that break up so many couples today: financial problems, disagreements, incompatibility, challenges of raising a family, and yes, just plain unhappiness.

Yet their commitment continued through the ins and outs because divorce wasn't an option. In their minds, there *was* no easy way out. And so instead of running away, they pushed through.

My Take on It

My goals for my marriage are that when we are eighty years old, we are sitting on the front porch in our rocking chairs looking at our grandchildren (and great-grandchildren), holding hands and whispering secrets to each other! Still able to kiss and hug and have a great time when we are together. This is so different from my parents' marriage because they have been divorced longer than I have been married.

—**Kristy, born in 1971**

Texas, married fifteen years

My biggest struggle with lifelong commitment is selfishness. Commitment takes compromise. Compromise takes sacrifice. Sacrifice takes humility and selflessness. Without humility, I cannot show grace and forgiveness. Without selflessness, my husband's needs and desires can never be met.

—**Michelle, born in 1971**

Ohio, married thirteen years

We Belong

...we belong together.

PAT BENATAR, BEST SHOTS, 1989, CAPITAL

"Don't want to leave you really," Pat Benatar sang in the popular eighties song "We Belong"—yet with half of all marriages today ending in divorce, her words hit a sour note for millions of couples each year.

So when did the generations start to think differently? When did divorce become an easy option? Sharon Jaynes talks about this in her book *Becoming the Woman of His Dreams*, quoting Pam Kelley.

> Since the 1960s, the women's liberation movement has made an attempt to make women become more like men by implying that being a woman isn't good enough. "We can do everything they can do—and even better," women have taunted, chanted, and cheered. Yes, we've come a long way, baby, and it's not looking too good. Since 1953, the divorce rate has climbed from 20 percent to the present 50 percent.[3]

The women's liberation movement accomplished a lot, but it worked to the detriment of one vital thing: respect for men. This word *respect* is one that's causing a lot of buzz lately in Christian marriage books, including *For Women Only* by Shaunti Feldhahn and *Love and Respect* by Dr. Emerson Eggerichs. And it's a word I, too, am learning to understand the importance of.

Through the 1960s, '70s, '80s, and beyond, women have proven that they can excel in every area of life, including politics and business. While I think this is wonderful (especially as a professional myself), some of our excelling has come at the cost of disrespecting men.

Think about it. In movies, on TV, and even in commercials, women are portrayed as smart and capable. Men, on the other hand, are the ones pulling them down or messing things up.

"While it may be totally foreign to most of us, the male need for respect and affirmation—especially from his woman—is so hardwired and so critical that most men would rather feel unloved than disrespected or inadequate," writes Shaunti Feldhahn in *For Women Only*.[4]

According to Feldhahn's survey, three out of four men agree with this. As a woman, this is hard to imagine, since a woman's driving need is to feel loved. Yet I suppose it makes sense. When you are disrespected, you feel lonely, unloved, and inadequate. I can only trust that God created men, including my husband, with this *vital need* for respect for a reason.

I've talked with my friends and, more important, my husband about this to see if it is a real need. Incredibly, a hunger for respect is more right-on than I ever realized. At work my husband receives kudos for a job well done. His paycheck and bonuses substantiate his skill and dedication. John works hard to provide for and protect his family.

Respecting John means admiring his work, his character, and his care. It's telling him that I appreciate these things and esteem him for being the man that he is. It's not talking negatively about him to my friends or even in a heart-to-heart with a close friend. Instead, it's "talking him up" at home and around others. It means not second-guessing his ideas. It's about honoring his opinions and decisions. (Which is tough when our opinions differ!)

Basically, it's my job as a wife to go against society and so-called liberated thinking and figure out how to unconditionally respect and honor my husband.

What does respect have to do with lifetime commitment? Everything. After all, why would a woman want to stick with a man she can't respect? And why would a man want to stay around when he's treated like the one who messes up all the time? Marriage is about more than this, of course. We made a covenant before God, and God has called us to commit for life. We'll talk about this too. But just think how we can transform our marriages, and our generation, when we strive to follow this principle.

Of course, God knew all along what we're just beginning to understand. Check out Ephesians 5:33: "Each one of you also must love his wife as he loves himself, and the wife must respect her husband."

Sadly, unconditional respect is something that generations of women have forgotten how to give. It's not that we wives purposefully set out to sabotage our marriages; but this is what lack of respect does. We tell our husbands we want them to be spiritual leaders and the head of the house, but then we make all the decisions…or question the decisions they do make. (*Ouch!* I've done this too many times to count.)

If we're going to strive for "forever," we need to think of ways to make this thing last. This is where hard work and planning are critical and vital.

A good question to ask yourself is, *How can I show my husband the respect he desires?* In my efforts to show John respect, I deliberately take time to affirm his capabilities, understand his point of view, and support his accomplishments. John especially appreciates it when I stop what I'm doing to give him a pat on the back after he mows the front lawn, cleans the garage, or builds a set of bookshelves. When I first started this practice, it felt like a mom talking to a three-year-old: "Great job, honey." But I quickly learned that he was energized by my praise.

The amazing thing about showing your husband respect is that when you deliberately look for ways to respect him and then put in the effort to accomplish those goals, your needs are met in the process. This is because when your husband gets the respect he needs, he in turn pours out his love.

Emerson Eggerichs, in his book *Love and Respect*, labels this the energizing cycle: "His love motivates her respect; her respect motivates his love."[5] I can personally confirm that being in this cycle is indeed energizing…not to mention fun!

So why is *respect* still such a foreign word, even to those of us who know its power? One reason could be that many of us weren't raised seeing it lived out. To place it within a more culture-friendly context, you might say that another word for respect is *admiration*. Here is how Dictionary.com defines them both:

Respect: -*noun*. Esteem for or a sense of the worth or excellence of a person, a personal quality or ability, or something considered as a manifestation of a personal quality or ability.

Admiration: -*noun*. A feeling of wonder, pleasure or approval.

What do you think a man would give to have a wife who respects and admires him? The answer is one that I've seen lived out in John's life, and it is this: *his whole heart*.

Sure, you might appreciate the idea of having your husband carry that twinkle in his eye for you thirty years from now, but what would you do to make his eyes twinkle today?

It's a question I have to ask myself every day. And then, even though it takes time and energy (both of which I seem to lack!), I need to act on the answers I come up with. Following through with my respectful and admiring ideas does take work, but it also increases the love in my marriage. This in turn makes "together forever" possible—for the years to come and also for today.

MY TAKE ON IT

Often Dan doesn't want help, just respect. Little things like letting him control the thermostat are *huge*.

—Angela, born in 1977

Idaho, married seven years

I have made an effort to forgive my husband of his faults and release him from my expectations. As a wife, I tend to have certain ideas about how things should be. This places expectations on my husband that he doesn't even know about. If he doesn't live up to those expectations, I tend to feel angry or hurt, when he doesn't even know what the problem is. I need to release my husband from those expectations and allow him to be who God created him to be (even making allowances for his faults).

—Michelle, born in 1971

Ohio, married thirteen years

Several years ago we renewed our vows. No, it wasn't a big, exciting shindig. We were actually on vacation in Las Vegas. And what do you do in Las Vegas? You get married, of course. The really surprising thing for me was that the vow renewal—as campy as we tried to make it—was actually a lot more moving for me than our first wedding. I think when we get married, most of us don't truly understand what we're getting ourselves into (much like first-time parenting). So those promises the second time around, at our renewal service, were a lot more important. This time we really understood what we were promising, and yet we promised anyway.

—MD, born in1968

New Jersey, married eleven years

Respect is seeing my husband do something I might not agree with, but not tearing him down for it or holding it against him later. It's pumping him up in those areas where he excels. It's telling my kids, with my hubby within earshot, that I'm proud of their daddy. It's letting the world know that I married the most wonderful man on the planet, even if he does leave his socks on the floor or forgets things I think are important. In the grand scheme of life, what's really more important? And there's a God who is watching me to see if I am being the wife He's called me to be.

—Allison, born in 1974

Florida, married thirteen years

AND ONE MORE THING...
FROM COOL TO CONSERVATIVE

Caroline Overington has studied the differences between Gen Xers and Boomers. In the article "Gen X Keen on the ABCs of Raising Gen Y," she quotes Kay Hymowitz of the Manhattan Institute:

> Married Generation Xers are the most traditional, conservative group in the country. They are much more traditional than their Boomer parents. I think we are seeing a backlash against the Boomers, who raised their kids in an era where there was a lot of divorce. A lot of Gen Xers suffered during that period and they are determined to do it differently for their own kids.[6]

What are Gen Xers backlashing against?

> A new generation [of Boomers] brought new beliefs and new ways, and its impact in the mid-1970s was so notable because that new generation was so large.... The early Boomers witnessed the arrival of television as a common fixture in almost every home. They experienced television's pervasive and often corrosive influences, but not when they were youngsters, not during the years when their outlook on life was being shaped. Younger Boomers grew up in the constant presence of television, and the more frequent and more explicit depictions of sex and violence held little shock value for them....
>
> The Baby Boom generation...made acceptable what previous genera-tions had rejected. Their attitudes toward sex, marriage, parenting, and divorce generally differed from that of their parents. Many of them viewed the use of drugs less harshly. Although many women regarded it desirable to find a husband or live-in partner in college, unlike most of their mothers they also had careers in mind. The careers might be interrupted by child-bearing, but not too soon and not too often.[7]

4 UNDER Pressure

Finding Balance

Insanity laughs under pressure we're cracking...

QUEEN AND DAVID BOWIE, HOT SPACE, 1981, EMI/ELEKTRA

Today is my husband's birthday—the big four-oh. In the midst of our busy lives, we were able to carve out one hour by ourselves followed by an ice-cream party with our kids and a few friends. It's sad really that right now my calendar is so packed that my dear hubby has to be scheduled between Monday night company and Wednesday night church.

If you ask any Gen Xer, finding balance in life is one of the things we struggle with most. It is also one of our greatest desires.

The Boomers' permissive style of parenting left their children, the Xers, so much to their own devices that Xers were labeled the "latchkey generation"—the first generation of kids who routinely came home to empty houses after school. Now Xers are in turn making extraordinary efforts to create a balance between work and home so that they can be with their families.[1]

The bottom line is that we greatly value our time spent with family. When we can't find that middle ground, we are stressed!

Sadly, our hurried and hectic lives probably do the most harm to our marriages. Instead of intimate partners, we become more like roommates—balancing schedules and juggling responsibilities. Some days I spend more time IMing my husband than talking face-to-face. Many nights we can be found sitting side by side on the couch, working in silence on our laptops. It's our version of quality time…*sort of*.

Sometimes I imagine what life was probably like before all this. Because I live in rural Montana, I can drive just a short ways out of town and come across abandoned homestead cabins. Those cabins were home to some of the first settlers in our community and were built before highways, handy marts, and hamburger joints.

Our five generations—GIs, Silents, Boomers, Xers and Millennials—have lived during the fastest moving century the world has ever known. During the past hundred years we walked on the moon, used the atom bomb and discovered the secrets of DNA. Television, the Internet, and cellphones turned the planet into a global village.[2]

Amazing, isn't it, how quickly things change? And it doesn't look as though the world will slow down anytime soon. Yet even in our busy lives, we can strive to do two things: (1) live a balanced life *in the midst of the hurried world around us*, and (2) hold on to age-old values and timeless traditions so they won't be lost for good.

Of course, no one is going to help us. Our balance must come from within, or we can be sure we'll live without it. We can also be sure that the faster we run, the more likely our marriages will limp along.

That's why John and I have chosen to prioritize the following things:

1 We don't sign up for any activity—for ourselves or our kids—before we talk about it together and look at the calendar. Sure, there are tons of fun, educational, and worthwhile pursuits out there, but each one we choose to pursue is time spent away from each other.

2 We have family dinners together 99 percent of the time. If John's running late getting home from work, the rest of us wait for him. Not only do we enjoy eating together, but seeing each other's faces around the table is like exhaling a big breath after a long day. It's refreshing.

3. We attend church together on Sunday mornings and Wednesday nights. If one of us has to go early, we go together. Sure, we could take two cars, but where's the fun in that?

4 We spend most of our evenings side by side. This includes walks, time spent talking, watching movies, and yes, working on our laptops next to each other. We also head to bed at the same time, even though one of us *(yawn)* gets tired an hour before the other.

These are simple areas in which balance works for us. Your list most likely will be different. The point is that you make one—that you decide which areas of your life you desire to preserve and protect. Because if *you* don't, no one else is going to do it for you.

My Take on It

Our schedule tends to be frantic. We go through cycles of normalcy, but with two and a half careers, grad school, ministry at church, and a child who's entered the activities stage (way too early, if you ask me), our schedule spirals out of control despite our best efforts. The crazier our schedule, the more stressed our relationship feels. It's hard to find time to devote to each other with everything else that pulls on our attention and time.

—Cara, born in 1974
Indiana, married eleven years

We learned a great lesson—balance does not mean that every day your time is spread equally between family, work, church, fun, friends, etc. Balance is how it all comes out in the end, and the overall feeling we have from week to week. My husband works full-time and is working on his PhD. I am a full-time mom of a toddler and one on the way. I also volunteer with several parenting groups. There are some weeks when we will not see each other except for a short hello, but there are other weeks when family time gets all the attention. We have learned how to check in with each other and monitor our "balance scale."

—Koryn, born in 1978

Indiana, married six years

My schedule is *very* chaotic, and it affects our marriage by adding stress to our day and bodies. Since we don't take our stressful frustrations out on our co-workers and acquaintances throughout the day, we are more irritable toward our spouse at the end of the day.

—Lesley, born in 1979

California, married eight years

Into the Groove

Get up on your feet, yeah, step to the beat.

MADONNA, *YOU CAN DANCE*, 1987, SIRE LONDON/RHINO

Recently, I was inspired while reading an article in *Time* magazine titled "Why We Worry About the Things We Shouldn't…and Ignore the Things We Should":

We pride ourselves on being the only species that understands the concept of risk, yet we have a confounding habit of worrying about mere possibilities while ignoring probabilities, building barricades against perceived dangers while leaving ourselves exposed to real ones…. We put filters on faucets, install air ionizers in our homes and lather ourselves with antibacterial soap…. At the same time, 20% of all adults still smoke; nearly 20% of drivers and more than 30% of backseat passengers don't use seat belts; two-thirds of us are overweight or obese.[3]

How does this concept apply to marriage? For starters, we're prone to spending a great deal of time and energy caring for people other than our spouse. We serve on church committees, join book clubs, or answer dozens of e-mails every day. Yet oftentimes we don't make the effort to shower our spouse with love and affection, to talk about our future dreams and goals, or to...well, we'll get to sex in a later chapter!

I'm often guilty of focusing on the wrong thing. I worry about what my neighbor thinks of the weeds growing in my flowerbed while ignoring the fact I haven't had a heart-to-heart conversation with John in weeks. I spend an hour decorating cookies for the church bake sale and then tell my family to fend for themselves when it comes to dinner.

"Our choices reveal what we love the most, what we fear, what is of ultimate value to us, and what we think we need in life—in other words, our choices expose the dominant desires of our heart," writes Leslie Vernick in *How to Act Right When Your Spouse Acts Wrong.*[4]

To put it another way, as Jesus said, "What will it profit a man if he gains the whole world, and loses his own soul?" (Mark 8:36, NKJV). What does it profit my family if I make the best school lunches, volunteer at the local rest home, or exercise daily—but lose touch with the person I committed to love forever?

The answer lies is recognizing the importance of balance in our marriage, then seeking to establish that balance. It's saying no to things we'll forget about next month anyway, with the goal of saying yes more often to our spouse: *Yes, let's have lunch together. Yes, I'd love to join you on that business trip. Yes, let's head to bed early...*

My Take on It

When my husband and I don't see each other very much, we fight a lot more. Often, he has to work late or attend late meetings at church. He feels guilty for not being home and becomes defensive. I feel rejected because he chose work and meetings over me, and I become hypersensitive. Rather than relishing the little time we have together, we end up hurt, angry, and disappointed.

Though we still struggle in this area, we both make an effort to serve one another in little ways. It helps to stay connected and committed. He rubs my feet in bed. I kiss him every time he comes home, no matter how late. He calls me from work just to say hi. I leave him little love notes in his car. It is the little things that make a big statement. We may not have a lot of free time, but we make time to show one another that we care.

—Michelle, born in 1971

Ohio, married thirteen years

We grew apart, and it seemed that we were actually leading separate lives until we had a marriage crisis. After the crisis, we both took a step back and realized that relationships always need work. They can never just be stagnant. It is important to make time for each other and recognize what the other's needs are. The biggest change we made was bringing the Lord into our relationship.

—Dee, born in 1975

Michigan, married ten years

Roll with It

Now there'll be a day, you'll get there baby…

Steve Winwood, Roll with It, 1988, Atlantic

The best way to find balance in life and in marriage is to make a plan. Too many times we set ourselves up for guilt and failure by saying yes to far more than we can complete successfully. We ignore that look in the eyes of our spouse that is pleading for a little attention (you know the one). We push ourselves with the promise that "after this is done, I'll take time for him/her…" while inwardly we know that the list will never be complete, and so does our spouse. In fact, a typical Gen X weakness of wanting to do too much makes a great first step. Here are a few more:

Say no to the unrealistic demands of others. "Pressures come from two directions: what other people expect of us and what we expect of ourselves," write Dennis and Barbara Rainey in *Staying Close*. "It is so easy to let yourself be driven by the agendas of other people. Externally, their voices form a deafening chorus, incessantly telling us what we ought to do."[5]

Realize the impact of fast-paced lives. "The persistent pressures of the pace we keep even make an impact on our health. According to the psychologist David Stoop, some forty million Americans suffer from allergies caused in part by pressure. Another thirty million have insomnia, twenty-five million have hypertension, and twenty million have ulcers. In addition, one out of three Americans has a weight problem, and all of this can be traced back, at least in part, to stress and pressure."[6]

> Every married couple I know of lives under the unending demands of pressures that cause them to be overcommitted, overextended, and overloaded.[7]

Make a plan for peace…realizing how much your spouse desires it. "Men often fantasize about a home life free of stress and worry. After work each day, his wife greets him lovingly at the door and his well-behaved children are also glad to see him. He enters the comfort of a well-maintained home as his wife urges him to relax before taking part in dinner, the aroma of which he can already smell wafting through the air," says Willard F. Harley, author of *His Needs, Her Needs*.

"Conversation at dinner is enjoyable and free of conflict," he continues. "Later the family goes out together for an early evening stroll, and he returns to put the children to bed with no hassle or fuss. Then he and his wife relax and talk together, watch a little television, and go to bed to make love, all at a reasonable hour."

Does that sound over the top? Listen to what else Harley has to say:

> Some wives may chuckle as they read the above scenario, but I assure you that if there is a wide gap between the reality of your home life and this fantasy, your marriage may be in serious trouble. A revolution in male attitudes in housework is supposed to have taken place, with men pitching in to take an equal share of the household chores. But this revolution has not necessarily changed

their emotional needs. Many of the men I counsel still tell me in private that they need domestic support as much as ever.[8]

Oddly enough, this scenario reminds me of the first time I traveled to Europe. I remember standing on the St. Charles Bridge in Prague on a beautiful spring day. Tourists snapped photos of the dozens of statues gracing the bridge. Men and women walked arm in arm, chatting in a language I didn't understand. At noon, church bells all over the city chimed in unison. I remember standing there and thinking, *I had no idea all this was possible. It's so much more wonderful than I ever imagined.*

I've had the same thought when John and I work together to balance our lives. We cut out things that won't matter ten years from now to focus on the things that will. Amazingly, we enjoy each other's company in the process. We also make time to laugh, talk, and dream. And I think to myself, *This is more wonderful than I ever imagined.*

Focus on one thing. Finally, it comes down to this:

The problem with most troubled marriages is that both partners are trying to accomplish far too many things in the world, and in the process, like Martha in Luke 10:42, they neglect the "one thing needful." Next to the love of God, the "one thing" that is by far the most important in the life of all married people is their marriage, their loving devotion to their partner. Nothing on earth must take precedence over that, not children, jobs, other friendships, not even "Christian work."...

Part of the secret to the effectiveness and strength of the peculiar little vows of marriage lies in this very scandal of waste, this extravagant simplicity of focus. For marriage involves nothing more than a lifelong commitment to love just one person—to do, whatever else one does, a good, thorough job of loving one person. What could be simpler than that? There is nothing simpler than love.[9]

A few months ago, I went through an exercise where I gave a gift to myself—something I wanted more than anything: a blank calendar. BLANK. And the joy of receiving this gift made me realize how much my crazy schedule was starting to get to me. It also helped me remember that *I am* in control. I can add or take off anything I like.

What a revelation!

Since then, I've been more purposeful about scheduling my time. I talk with John, and we block out time for vacation and fun. I write in date nights, my morning quiet time, and even certain days for errands. I talk with God and ask His opinion on how I spend my minutes. I pray over the numerous activities that beg to fill those white boxes—and because of prayer, many of them never make it on the page.

In other words, I plan for success instead of allowing myself to get caught up in a cycle of guilt and overcommitment. I have embraced this gift.

And now, I offer you same challenge. What will you do?

My Take on It

I've gotten to the point where I realize God's plan for my life is (1) real and (2) better than anything I can come up with on my own. It's liberating to know that I can let Him guide my steps each day since I don't have to worry about planning it all out myself. Unlike the bumper stickers you see from time to time that say "GOD IS MY COPILOT," I believe in "GOD IS MY PILOT; I'M HANGING OUT IN FIRST CLASS." I'd rather sit in that seat enjoying the ride than fly the plane any day.

—Chris, born in 1974

Florida, married thirteen years

And One More Thing...

The ideal American lifestyle has become inextricably linked to matrimony. The CEO icons of the new millennium, both male and female, contrast themselves favorably with the power-hungry bankers and single-minded career women of the eighties by proudly brandishing their wedding rings, family-friendly SUVs, and well-rounded lifestyles. They boast of achieving "balance" in their lives. When they discuss their goals and their values, they point out their overriding desire to get home to the kids at the end of the day....

In a 1999 poll, more Boomers than Gen Xers agreed with the following statement: "People should live for themselves rather than their children.... Today's [Gen Xers] show their parents that they are *not like them* by sidling up to the very institutions their parents neglected or debunked. And then they go one step further and prove they're better at the good life than their parents ever were." [10]

5

I Remember You

Overcoming the Bond of Past Relationships

Remember yesterday—walking hand in hand.

SKID ROW, *SKID ROW*, 1989, ATLANTIC

At age eighteen I walked down the aisle to where John waited. I looked like the perfect bride. I was adorned in a beautiful gown, carrying in my hands a bouquet of roses, a smile curling my lips as ruffles trailed behind me. But inside, I bore scars of past hurts—memories of embraces with past lovers, secret intimacies that had fulfilled me for a season.

I didn't truly understand the impact of those past relationships until years later. It took years for the layers of pain, doubt, longing, and loss to reveal them from where they lay buried. Even though I enjoyed a solid marriage, memories of past boyfriends surfaced at the oddest times. Sometimes in my dreams. Sometimes when I heard a certain song on the radio. At other times they appeared out of nowhere, like scenes from a movie replaying in my mind.

Shame was my first response, then guilt: *How can I let my mind go there?* Then an honest longing to leave the past in the past.

I turned to God. Pleaded with Him to wash away the thoughts and scrub off the layers of longings. But more often than not, I'd discover a toughened skin of memories and emotions beneath the surface of the one peeled away.

I sought forgiveness for many past mistakes from both God and myself. For losing my virginity in high school. For getting pregnant twice—having an abortion and later carrying a child at seventeen.

I dealt with each mistake on my knees. And while John was a faithful and caring husband, I believed only I could face these struggles. First, because it was *my* heart that had been wounded. Second, because I knew that God alone provided the source of true healing. And third, because there were things I didn't want to admit, even to John. He knew I'd been pregnant twice, but he knew little about those past relationships. He knew I'd been hurt and abandoned, but I knew in order to explain the impact of those circumstances, I'd have to bare my soul. *No thanks.*

Instead, it felt easier to keep everything hidden away and tucked inside. Easier to simply carry my tears and prayers to God, who knew everything and still loved me.

So that's the way we lived for years. With me holding back and believing that John might not love me as much if he "knew the whole truth." And with John always feeling as if I'd never given him my whole heart.

The fact was, I hadn't.

The years passed: five, ten, fifteen. We enjoyed a happy marriage and a good life, and I experienced many levels of healing. I helped a local crisis pregnancy center get started and began mentoring teen moms. I led Bible studies through which other women were freed from the pain of their past.

In my ignorance, I felt I'd finally done all the right things, followed God on the correct path, and could now be a good example for others to follow. (A little prideful, don't you think?)

In fact, one morning during my devotion I honestly believed I could stand boldly before God, pure and complete—knowing that, through Christ, I was in right standing with my Maker. I'd confessed my sins to God, and I lived a passionate life of service. I believed I'd forgiven those who'd hurt me, and I'd finally come to a place where the past lived in the past. For good.

Yet still, I wanted to know if there was anything else offensive in me, so I prayed aloud the psalm in that day's devotion:

Search me, O God, and know my heart;
  Try me and know my anxious thoughts;
And see if there be any hurtful way in me,
  And lead me in the everlasting way. (Psalm 139:23–24, NASB)

The answer came the next day, and it rocked me to my core.

My Take on It

I was never taught sexual purity. However, my mom did offer to get me on birth control when the time was right. I had several sexual relationships in my dating years. So did my husband. The days early in our relationship lacked the adventure and mystery of courting. Instead we jumped right in to living together. Our marriage, therefore, started with doubt and jealousy. We always had the previous experiences in our minds, and it took years to overcome the baggage and heartache that came with it. I gave away my purity long before I knew what a treasure it was.

—**Michelle, born in 1971**
Ohio, married thirteen years

How do those past relationships affect my marriage? I have scars from the past that have made some parts of me calloused or defensive. I have wounds that are healing, and it makes our marriage uncomfortable. I am suspicious of my husband—that he is gonna treat me the way I was treated (badly). I have sinned, and now I'm reaping the fruit of those sins, and it causes pain today for others.

—**Katie, born in 1972**
Montana, married seven years

Sometimes we are caught up in the thrill of something different, new, maybe better from someone other than our spouse, which is how so many affairs get started and get out of hand. It's the pull of someone attracted to you—desiring you. It makes you feel special, loved. It's the feeling we all crave. I know because I've been there, but when it came right down to it, it was just me giving in to temptation and being selfish. Sin. And I hurt my husband terribly. Talk about regret.

—Anne, born 1973

Washington, married twelve years

The One That You Love

Here I am, the one that you love, askin' for another day.

 Air Supply, *The One That You Love*, 1981, Buddha Records

I had a smile on my face as I worked on my latest writing project. After all, life was good. My kids were excelling in many areas. My husband's job was going great, and we were very devoted to each other. My career seemed to be taking off with the completion of my fourth World War II novel, and I had signed contracts for five more books—three fiction and two nonfiction. Life couldn't get any better.

Then an e-mail showed up in my inbox. Just seeing the name of the sender got my heart pounding. The e-mail contained only a few lines: "Hi, Tricia. I've been thinking about you and looking for you for a while. Remember me?"

Remember? How could I forget?

The e-mail was from my first love. The person I'd lost my virginity to. The person I'd always thought I'd marry someday. The person who had entered my mind often.

I e-mailed back. "Uh, yes, I remember you. How are you?" My response sounded innocent enough, but I should have known from my quivering fingers that opening a line of communication was a mistake. After all, how would I feel if one of John's old girlfriends popped up out of thin air? Yeah, I wouldn't like *that* much.

Still, I was curious. What had Steven been up to? What had happened in his life? Was he married?

But mostly...why was he still thinking about me?

I remembered the last time I saw him. I'd been married for a few years and had run into him in town with his girlfriend and their baby daughter. "Oh, what's her name?" I had asked, making small talk and noticing how much the baby looked like her handsome daddy.

"Tricia," he answered with a twinkle in his eyes.

I gave Steven a disbelieving look.

He shrugged. "Hey, I like the name," he said with a smile.

Fifteen years later, as I stared at my inbox waiting for his response, this memory and many others filled my mind.

One e-mail response turned into two. Then three. Then ten. Next came a phone call.

Talking to Steven felt as if twenty years hadn't passed. We talked about our careers and our marriages. (Mine was happy; his wasn't.) We talked about our kids. We talked about his out-of-town move that put a halt to our relationship during high school. And Steven talked about his thoughts of me over the years.

By this time, I knew I was in *big* trouble. I loved John, but I was extremely flattered by Steven's admiration. (Who wouldn't be?) Not only that, it felt good—really good—to be pursued. To think that I'd been treasured in his thoughts all these years. To realize that with one phone call, he trusted me enough to confide in me again. And that he still cared after all these years.

What scared me the most was how badly I wanted to keep talking to him. Only two days after receiving the first e-mail, I felt caught up in a whirlwind of emotion. How could this happen so fast?

I prayed for God to rescue me from myself, but the desire to keep our communication a secret ruled my mind and emotions. *Warning! Warning!* Through the forceful prodding of God's Holy Spirit within me, I knew what I had to do. It was time to call in backup.

My Take on It

I have a lot of past relationships, and my dear husband essentially has none. This dichotomy would affect our marriage if we let it. Fortunately, God led me on a huge journey of healing before my husband and I even started dating. Now when the past comes back to haunt me or condemn me (and these times are more and more rare), the closer my husband and I get. I just give it to God again and claim His grace and forgiveness.

—Jessica H., born in 1975

Iowa, married four years

I think my past relationships have brought a great deal of shame into my life and into my marriage. The struggles involve trust issues and self-esteem issues. Also, since I have been unable to have a child with my husband, I wonder sometimes if he wouldn't have been better off with another, more capable woman.

—Ann, born in 1965

Texas, married twelve years

Somebody Save Me

Saaaaaaave me...

CINDERELLA, NIGHT SONGS, 1986, MERCURY

Past memories and renewed emotions coursed through me as I communicated with Steven. I knew I needed to (1) stop all communication with Steven and (2) tell John. But to do both, I needed help.

Thankfully, I'm blessed with a network of online writer friends. Some have been my prayer partners for twelve years via e-mail, others more recently. Yet these strong, faithful, God-loving women are the ones I turn to when the going gets tough. They diligently hold me up in prayer, and they aren't afraid to give me a strong rebuke when one is needed. Which it was in this case.

Within minutes of e-mailing my urgent request ("Help…an old boyfriend popped up, and I *really* like talking to him!"), the prayers, support, and advice came flooding in.

Yes, they understood the seriousness of the situation. Yes, they said they would pray. Yes, they urged me to cut off communication with Steven and tell John. And yes, they would hunt me down and tie me up if I didn't promise to do the right thing!

Though I didn't want to hurt my husband, I knew my warrior prayer-sisters were right. I needed John's accountability. I needed his love to help me turn my back on the person who still held part of my heart—even after so many years.

Telling John wasn't easy. I had to begin by telling him *who* Steven was. John hadn't asked much about my past relationships, and I hadn't filled him in. Sobs poured from me as I told him about this relationship at a young age, about the sexual intimacy, and about my memories and feelings, which obviously hadn't dissipated over time.

John listened. He cried, and he took me in his arms and confessed his love for me. Then he prayed over me. He prayed that God would heal me and help me do the right thing. John prayed for his own strength too. He prayed for *our* wounded hearts. He prayed that God would help us face this battle together and come out stronger at the end.

And truth be told, when I confessed *everything* to my husband and witnessed intense love in his gaze…I have never loved John more. At that moment, I also understood God's love deeper than I ever had.

My Take on It

My past relationships made it very difficult to trust my husband. I'd been date raped and dumped, so trusting a male ranked high on my "DO NOT DO" list. I think godly Christian counseling helped our marriage the most was. Through some incredible counselors we've been able to work through twelve years of a rocky marriage and our past hurts before we met so that we're on a different path now. We're growing as individuals and as a couple—whole, full, and increasingly healthier.

—Amy W., born in 1970

Georgia, married twelve years

My husband's past relationship has been hard to deal with because he and an old girlfriend had what he calls a "perfect year." I always feel as though I am trying to live up to their relationship.

—Dee, born in 1975

Michigan, married ten years

I didn't have many relationships in high school because my parents were so very strict. My husband was quite promiscuous and was something of a bad boy in high school—and that has affected me by giving me something else to be insecure about. It was really something that we needed to talk through, and I required a lot of reassurance from him. It's not something that even comes up anymore.

—Amy P., born in 1971

South Carolina, married five years

Breaking the Chains

I broke the chains. So let me be. I've gotta be free.

DOKKEN, BREAKING THE CHAINS, 1981, ELEKTRA RECORDS

I wish I could say that my connection with Steven ended there, but it didn't. A few more e-mails were exchanged—namely, the one in which I told him that communication between us *had* to stop. There was another phone call too—a moment of weakness. I wanted to hear his voice…one last time.

More talks with friends. More weeping with John. More prayers. Many, many more prayers. And finally, lots of accountability. Friends who forced me to tell them the truth. And my husband, who asked that I confess my thoughts, emotions, and temptations every night before we fell asleep.

Second Peter 2:9 says, "The Lord knows how to rescue the godly from temptation" (NASB). It was *this* truth and many more that rescued me.

From my first e-mail seeking help, my friends not only prayed, but they also sent me Scripture verses to read. I clung to them like a lifeline, printing them from e-mails and writing them in my journal. It was truth that brought freedom. Here are a few that spoke to my heart during this time:

> Since you have heard all about him and have learned the truth that is in Jesus, throw off your old evil nature and your former way of life, which is rotten through and through, full of lust and deception. Instead, there must be a spiritual renewal of your thoughts and attitudes. You must display a new nature because you are a new person, created in God's likeness—righteous, holy, and true. (Ephesians 4:21–24, NLT)

> Blessed is the [wo]man who perseveres under trial, because when [s]he has stood the test, [s]he will receive the crown of life that God has promised to those who love him. (James 1:12)

> Forgetting the past and looking forward to what lies ahead, I strain to reach the end of the race and receive the prize for which God, through Christ Jesus, is calling us up to heaven. (Philippians 3:13–14, NLT)

I read these Scriptures and turned them into prayers from my heart. I also wrote in my journal, using them as a launching point. I wrote about the lies I had clung to from the past…and the truth found in Christ.

It is so important to rehearse these truths daily:

* The truth about love. What it is and what it isn't.
* The truth about emotions. We can do the right thing despite our emotions.
* The truth about an intimate marriage. Intimacy is sharing our hearts and our struggles with the one whom we've vowed to love for life.

I wish I could say that now, a year later, thoughts of Steven are a thing of the past. But that isn't the case. The memories are still there. The emotions haven't faded completely. And some days I still face the temptation of my e-mail and phone.

But I *choose* to be faithful. As soon as a memory or a thought surfaces, I turn it over to God in prayer. I also ask John to pray for me. Together we ask God to use this temptation to strengthen us and our marriage.

And it has. I can truly say that John and I talk about everything more often. We know each other's hearts better than we ever have.

Why Me?

I found so much more.

IRENE CARA, WHAT A FEELIN', 1983, NETWORK

When this first happened, I was mad at God. *Why would You let this happen, Lord? Why did You have to test me like this? Why did You have to make it hurt so much—not just hurt my heart, but John's also?*

And in the gentle way God speaks, I received my answer—not through an audible voice but in an inner knowing.

You asked Me to search your heart and reveal the areas still unclaimed by Me. I brought to the surface what you chose to ignore all these years. There was rebuilding that needed to be done. It was time for the lies of the past to be demolished and for your ideas of love to be rebuilt upon Truth.

Through this, God also showed me the reality of 1 Corinthians 10:13: "No temptation has seized you except what is common to man. And God is faithful; he will not let you be tempted beyond what you can bear. But when you are tempted, he will also provide a way out so that you can stand up under it."

Of course, through this experience I learned that the "way out" wasn't that Steven drop off the face of the planet. Or that all my memories be erased. Or every emotion stilled.

Instead, the way out involved reaching out to trusted friends, lying on my face before God in prayer, claiming the truth of God's Word, and turning for help to the person I'd promised to love and cherish all the days of my life.

"Why me?" Irene Cara sang.

"For I know the plans that I have for you," declares the Lord, "plans for welfare and not for calamity to give you a future and a hope." (Jeremiah 29:11, NASB)

And that's something worth clinging to.

AND ONE MORE THING...

"Cutting ties with former lovers is like removing the big, obvious boxes in your basement. Once you've given these to God, the heavy work is done; the majority of your basement is clean."[1]

"Old flames will flicker as long as the mind can consider what might have been. But you didn't choose the old flame, nor did your partner. You chose each other. You chose because you were ready for something more than transience. You sought transformation. A gift such as this naturally demands something in return: your daily presence—physical and emotional—in your marriage. Your marriage is only 'there' to the extent that you are.

"Don't wait for old flames to die. Instead, realize that both of you are playing in a much bigger game, for stakes that involve your very lives. Respect what each of you has willingly risked."[2]

6
IN Your EYES

Intimacy

...I am complete.

PETER GABRIEL, *SO*, 1986, GEFFEN RECORDS

s I spoke about in the last chapter, I explored my sexuality at a young age. For our generation of Gen Xers, the themes behind movies and music, videos and television, revolved around finding love and having sex. It *seemed* like the normal thing to do. Madonna sang, "Like a virgin…," but no one talked about remaining one or saving themselves for marriage. On *Days of Our Lives*, Bo and Hope were friends *and lovers*, and it was all my friends and I could talk about. My own virginity is something I gave away when I was barely in high school.

Intimacy, on the other hand, has been more of a struggle. And not just sexual intimacy, but making heart connections that count.

Growing up, I learned to entertain myself with TV and books. I found it easier to be alone than to interact with difficult family members. I had close relationships with my friends…but not too close. In high school, I got together with guys and then broke up, each time guarding myself a little more.

I'm not the only Gen Xer who struggles with intimacy issues. As a generation, we learned to exist on the surface but not go too deep. Listen to this:

While some factors are more significant than others, perhaps the most significant element in value development is age. Many psychologists and sociologists would agree that the most influential period of our value-development process is around age ten. What happened to you and what was going on in society when you were ten years old has shaped your values probably more than you realize.... What we experienced in our families, at school, with our friends, through the media, and in every aspect of our lives at age ten had a greater influence on us than those same factors had at any other time in our lives.[1]

This explanation makes a lot of sense to me. When I was ten years old, my parents were struggling in their relationship, and many of my friends' parents were already divorced. Communication between me and my family consisted of safe topics like school or chores. I could sense financial strain. I attended church, but I didn't really know God. I was an obedient kid, but I was just going through the motions of life.

Later, when my mom and stepdad divorced, it confirmed what I had already learned: Keep your guard up, and don't let anyone in completely. That was the only way you wouldn't get hurt.

Contrary to what we have long thought, the major impact of divorce does not occur during childhood or adolescence. Rather, it rises in adulthood as serious romantic relationships move center stage. When it comes time to choose a life mate and build a new family, the effects of divorce crescendo. A central finding to my research is that children identify not only with their mother and father as separate individuals but with the relationship between them. They carry the template of this relationship into adulthood and use it to seek the image of their new family. The absence of a good image negatively influences their search for love, intimacy, and commitment. Anxiety leads many into making bad choices in relationships, giving up hastily when problems arise, or avoiding relationships altogether.[2]

Intimacy has represented one of the biggest struggles in my marriage to John. Even before last year and the experience with Steven, I felt as if I had a whole separate part of me, deep inside, that John knew nothing about. I would share my feelings with him as long as they didn't present conflict—but if I thought they had the smallest chance of causing conflict, I avoided the discussion. It was easier for me to put on a happy face than pour out my heart.

As couples, we choose to marry because we want to enjoy a heart connection with another person for life. That's why I married John. But it was hard to make that connection when my heart was surrounded by a solid wall.

One definition of intimacy I really like is this: *"into me see."* But letting someone else see into your soul is possible only when you practice transparency—sharing with your spouse the truth about past conflicts, former relationships, and personal struggles both past and present.

I resisted transparency even after sixteen years of marriage because I was afraid to let John know how sinful I really am. I was sure he'd hate me if he knew about my wild high school years (although I don't know why I thought that). Of course, he knew about certain things—such as my teen pregnancy—but I never told him about other relationships I had with different guys. I was certain he'd be horrified by my day-to-day struggles, such as thinking a guy friend from church was cute (horrible, I know!) or how my heart pounded during a romantic movie.

Over the years, it grew easier to keep things to myself than risk seeing disappointment or pain in my husband's gaze.

I realize today that even though I've been in a committed relationship since I was eighteen, I feared love. Nearly every example of love I had seen was warped. After all, I witnessed what "love" did to my own parents. I felt its effects in broken high school relationships.

"Ironically, the best way to defeat our fear of love is to choose to love. God's Word offers this encouragement in 1 John 4:18. 'There is no fear in love. But perfect love drives out fear, because fear has to do with punishment. The one who fears is not made perfect in love,'" writes Jen Abbas, author of *Generation Ex.* "Fear is self-centered: What will *they* do? Love is other-focused: What can *I* do?"

Abbas goes on to say:

> The decision to love is a willingness to *engage*. The love that is most satisfying—that which is reciprocated—is also beyond our control. In order for someone to get to know us well enough to love us, we must be willing to contradict our coping mechanisms—we must be trusting, vulnerable, and willing to relinquish control.
>
> We may be able to accept an intellectual belief that God empowers us to love. But love that is based in knowledge alone will only guilt-trip or shame us into acting right. However, we can ask God to help us connect the dots from our head to our heart.[3]

Abbas's directive is right-on. Over time I've worked to reveal myself to John, layer by layer. It's a process, but I'm seeing its effects on our intimacy level. I feel loved after I bare all; I witness love in my husband's gaze.

The following things helped me as I peeled away the layers:

1. **I understood that my wall of protection was a coping mechanism.** God created us with an innate ability to cope during difficult circumstances. But I was nearly two decades into a loving, committed relationship when I realized that my fear was a coping mechanism I no longer needed. After all, my issues and insecurities came BC (before Christ) *and* before John.
2. **I realized I did not need to feel guilty for my lack of intimacy.** Guilt never helped me connect. In fact, it just pushed me farther from a resolution. Instead, I started looking ahead to the hope and freedom found in connecting with my spouse.
3. **I discovered where the fear came from.** We have an enemy of our souls who will use anything he can to keep us disconnected from God and from our spouses. I chose to believe God's promise. Second Timothy 1:7 says, "For God has not given us a spirit of fear, but of power and of love and of a sound mind" (NKJV).

4. **I found out that God could help.** The closer I grew to God, the more I understood the barriers I'd erected around my heart. Yet God did not leave me to tear them down alone, but worked within me as only He can.

As Abbas said, we can ask God to "help us connect the dots from our head to our heart." I didn't want to let down my guard, so I prayed that God would help me release my fear—help me to engage. In return, God answered my prayers by softening all the hard parts of my soul.

I also discovered that I wasn't the only one praying. During the time I struggled to let John into my inner recesses, my husband was praying for God to show me His love. John prayed that his responses would draw us closer and make me more comfortable with intimacy in marriage.

Though I felt God's freedom to open myself up more and more to John—not keeping my internal life separate—it wasn't easy. One thing that helped the most was to talk in the dark of our bedroom. It also helped John to know that I didn't expect him to give me a response or solve anything. Simply feeling him by my side was enough…followed by his embrace and whispered affection when I was through spilling my guts.

"The wedding is merely the beginning of a lifelong process of handing over absolutely everything, and not simply everything that one owns but everything that one is," writes Mike Mason in *The Mystery of Marriage*.

There is no one who is not broken by this process. It is excruciating and inexorable, and no one can stand up to it. Everyone gets broken on the wheel of love, and the breaking that takes place is like nothing else under the sun.…

That is the vulnerable place in all human relationships. What is on the line, always, with every person we meet, is our capacity to love and to be loved. But whereas in most other relationships our vulnerability in this respect can be hidden, more or less (and how expert we are at hiding it!), in the relationship of marriage it is this very quality of vulnerability that is exposed, exalted, exploited. And this is the thing that can prove to be too much for people, too much to handle. Many give up and run away, their entire lives collapsing in ruins. But even those who hang on face inevitable ruin, for they must be broken too.[4]

I've learned that it's okay to be broken. To be vulnerable. To expose the deepest corners of one's heart. Opening myself to my God and my spouse is like popping the cork on a bottle and allowing its contents to gush out. The best part is that once those things are freed, then there is room for love.

My Take on It

While we were a close family growing up, we were never an intimate family. We loved one another, but we did not feel comfortable sharing our feelings and fears, our desires and doubts, our hopes and our hurts. We just weren't comfortable with the vulnerability that is necessary for intimacy. Over time, brick by brick, I built a wall of protection around myself. Also, the feelings of rejection and dismissal I felt after ending past relationships left me even more cautious in allowing myself to become vulnerable and exposed. Intimacy became something I feared rather than something I desired.

—Michelle, born in 1971

Ohio, married thirteen years

I have decided to humble myself and follow God, even with my husband. I have nothing to lose, so I just let it all be out there…I guess. It's weird because I don't think my husband really wants me to be transparent, unless it's something that is easy for him to deal with and/or makes him happy. We aren't really that close because of all our differences… Maybe all marriages are like this. I don't know.

—Katie, born in 1972

Montana, married seven years

My wife and I talk about everything, even the most embarrassing stuff. That vulnerability on both sides leads to the trust and transparency that's needed.

—Chris, born in 1974

Florida, married thirteen years

I Think We're Alone Now

There doesn't seem to be anyone around.

Tiffany, Tiffany, 1987, MCA

In high school, one of my favorite songs was sung by a young singer named Tiffany. "I think we're alone now," she sang as she described young lovers running off to be together.

To me, the image of two young lovers running away hand in hand invoked togetherness: Even if no one else in the world understood them, they understood each other. They wanted to be together to the exclusion of everyone else.

This desire is one we're all born with. "I believe God has placed in each human heart the desire to know and be known. We long for intimacy, even as children," says Sharon Jaynes in *Becoming the Woman of His Dreams*. "Little girls want a best friend with whom they can share secrets, hold hands, and write love notes. Little boys want a blood brother with whom they can make a secret pact, have a secret handshake, and play catch. While we may have glimpses of intimate friendship throughout our lives, it is only through the marriage relationship, wherein a man and a woman become one flesh, that true intimacy can be realized."[5]

Running away hand in hand was also an image of acceptance. And how many of us during those preteen and teen years felt truly accepted?

A man may lose himself among many gods, but to accept the one true Lord is to allow himself to be found. Similarly in marriage the acceptance of one permanent partner turns out, in a profound way, *to be an acceptance of oneself*. For the closer we are drawn into the brilliant and mysterious circle of another person, the more must we ourselves be revealed in the other's light, revealed for what we are. Others are mirrors in which we are constrained to see ourselves, not as we would like to be, but as we are. Whenever we pull away, searching in one mirror after another for a more pleasing image, what we are really doing is avoiding the truth about ourselves (emphasis mine).[6]

Intimacy, then, is discovering the truth about ourselves. When I hid my inner feelings from John, it was easy to pretend they didn't exist. Having to reveal my weaknesses, hopes, fears, and struggles made them real—not only to my husband, but to me as well.

The same word picture of running hand in hand is described in the most romantic book in the Bible, Song of Songs:

> Let him kiss me with the kisses of his mouth—
> for your love is more delightful than wine.
> Pleasing is the fragrance of your perfumes;
> your name is like perfume poured out.
> No wonder the maidens love you!
> Take me away with you—let us hurry!
> Let the king bring me into his chambers. (Song of Songs 1:2–4)

These three verses remind us again of God's intention from the beginning: exclusiveness to each other. Unfortunately, the more common scenario today is husbands and wives who exclude themselves, and their hearts, from one another.

Husbands excluding wives and wives excluding husbands is exactly what happens when loneliness and isolation infect a marriage. When you're excluded, you have a feeling of distance, a lack of closeness, and little real intimacy. You can share a bed, eat at the same dinner table, watch the same

TV, share the same checking account, and parent the same children—and still be alone. You may have sex, but you don't have love; you may talk, but you do not communicate. You may live together, but you don't share your life with one another.[7]

Who wants to live like that?

I have only one suggestion: Take the first step toward knowing your spouse and being known. That step could be sharing a secret emotion with your spouse. It may be listening as he or she shares. Perhaps it is taking time to pray together. The step may be confessing your hang-ups to God…and then confessing them to your spouse.

I love the Chinese proverb that says, "The journey of a thousand miles begins with but a single step." The same can be said about the journey toward intimacy in our marriages.

Won't you start today?

MY TAKE ON IT

With much prayer, I am learning to allow myself to become vulnerable. I must expose all of me in order to allow God to change me. I must first be broken. This intimacy with the Lord helps me become more intimate with my husband.

—Michelle, born in 1971

Ohio, married thirteen years

I have learned that it is okay to be who I am with my husband. He doesn't judge me for my past mistakes; he doesn't judge me for mistakes I make today. I can just be the real me, and that is okay with him. That makes me feel *safe*.

—Kristy, born in 1971

Texas, married fifteen years

And One More Thing...

For many Xers, the marriage pattern they saw as they were growing up was divorce. That scared them to the degree that they tend to wait longer to get married and are hesitant to get into a marriage situation that could end in divorce. The trend of couples living together without being married (started by the Boomers) continues to be a real option in many Xers' minds.[8]

In 1980, the divorce rate had grown from one in three (1970) to one in two; one-parent families had increased 50 percent; unmarried couples living together were up 300 percent; and one million teenagers became pregnant, two-thirds of them unmarried.[9]

In 1988, two-parent families made up only 27 percent of the population, compared to 49 percent in 1970. Since 1980, the number of singles was up 20 percent, unmarried couples 63 percent.[10]

7 AGAINST All ODDS

Media Matters

You're the only one who really knew me at all.

PHIL COLLINS, *Face Value*, 1981, VIRGIN/ATLANTIC

I have a love-hate relationship with the media. I love it, but I also hate that I love it.

I love the variety of music, television programs, and movies. I hate the influence it has on society and on me personally.

I love following the scoop on all the stars (*People* magazine, for example), but I also hate that I'm curious about the lives of Brad and Angelina or Britney and… whomever.

Is it just me?

Dr. Rick and Kathy Hicks write in *Boomers, Xers, and Other Strangers*:

The eighties were a rough time for kids to grow up. Their parents tended to be self-absorbed and distracted by things like making a living and finding their own fulfillment. There were many broken homes with single-parent families struggling to survive financially. A lot of kids were left to fend for themselves emotionally, if not physically. Latchkey kids (those who came home from school to an empty house) were common. Because of this, TV and movies (especially with the invention of the VCR) became an ever-increasing source of values input. Older kids looked to peers, even gangs, for a sense of belonging or for role models that were missing in their homes.[1]

This was certainly true for me. While I was growing up, *Romper Room, The Rocky and Bullwinkle Show,* and *Mister Rogers' Neighborhood* welcomed my day. I loved watching reruns of *The Brady Bunch* after school. ("Here's the story/Of a lovely lady…") Family favorites included *CHiPs* and *The Dukes of Hazzard.* (Oh, to be Daisy Duke!) The Smurfs and Bugs Bunny were my friends every Saturday morning.

Of course, these were mild cases of media influence. I also remember watching horror movies, such as *The Changeling.* It came out in 1980, when I was only nine. I remember watching it with my parents. Memories of that film still haunt me.

There were other movies, equally bad, that I watched through the crack in my bedroom door. In fact, when I put my pillow on the end of the bed, I had a perfect view of the TV from my room. Of course, I took advantage of that.

The false connection and drama caused by night after night of TV impacted me. The sex, violence, and attitudes did too. They still do.

"My yesterdays walk with me. They keep step, they are faces that peer over my shoulder," says Nobel Prize winner William Golding. I believe that. I also think that sometimes our yesterdays meet us through reruns on TV Land on Thursday nights at 7 p.m.

My Take on It

Each house in our neighborhood lives in its own little world, and if we are not careful, each member of our family can end up in their own little world. With each family member off in their own room either on a computer or watching their own separate TV, we can disconnect as a family. The same media that brings the world closer together can drive families farther apart.

—Jennifer, born in 1969

Wisconsin, married thirteen years

MTV and the radio were my friends! I was socially awkward most of my growing-up years, so these forms of musical and visual escape made me feel connected. The bad part about that was in watching TV instead of connecting in real life with other people, the social awkwardness didn't disappear; it only got worse. I also allowed what I viewed on MTV to define my morals. After becoming a Christian, the Lord had a lot of cleanup work to do in my mind with all the stuff I'd lived on for so long.

—Amy, born in 1970

Georgia, married twelve years

Looking back, I can't believe the television shows my mom let me watch. Media influenced my moral standards greatly. Promiscuity, marital affairs, crime, bullying, immodesty all became acceptable, fun, and even rewarding. Then I had children of my own. As I became aware of the negative influence of media on my children, I evaluated the influence media had had on my own morals and choices. I don't want my children to find acceptable all that the media portrays as innocent entertainment.

—Michelle, born in 1971

Ohio, married thirteen years

I Still Haven't Found
What I'm Looking For

...you know I believed it.

U2, Joshua Tree, 1987, Island Records

According to AC Nielsen, the average American watches more than four hours of TV each day (or twenty-eight hours per week, which is equivalent to two months of nonstop TV watching every year). In a sixty-five-year-long life, that person will have spent *nine years* glued to the tube. While I personally don't watch four hours of television a day, it is still a huge part of my world and my marriage.

Media choices are actually one place in which John and I don't always agree. In fact, as you'll see from the numerous comments from other Gen Xers, everyone has a different opinion on how media intake should be handled.

The best thing is to consider *your* marriage and family. What works best for you? What is God convicting you of? By talking through our thoughts, feelings, and convictions, John and I have learned to compromise. Here are a few things we've come up with:

No watching TV in your room at bedtime. According to Italian sexologist, Serenella Salomoni, you aren't getting as much sex as you could if you have a television in your bedroom: "If there's no television in the bedroom, the frequency [of sexual intercourse] doubles."[2] For us, no TV in our bedroom was an easy choice.

Talk about your feelings concerning media. I joked in an earlier chapter about writing out the verse "I will set before my eyes no vile thing" (Psalm 101:3). I mentioned writing it on a sticky note and sticking it to the remote control. I didn't actually do that. Instead, I stuck it right on the television.

When we first married and John would watch something I felt was inappropriate, I'd make a snide remark. Or make a face. Or leave the room. Or post a sticky note. John was better about it. When he didn't like something I was watching, he'd just turn the channel. (*Yeah, that went over well.*)

Over the last few years, we've tried to communicate what we like, or don't like, about certain programs. For example, growing up I loved watching the Miss America Pageant. My mom, grandma, and I would choose our favorites and then see whose girl won. One day when I turned it on, John started complaining. Come to find out, watching beautiful women parade around a stage for two hours was a huge temptation for a guy. God made men visual, after all, and it got his thoughts heading in all sorts of directions. Once John explained this to me, turning the channel was an easy choice.

Likewise, I've talked to John about some of the violence on TV that bothers me. Sure, crime shows are interesting to try to solve as you watch, but some of the gory images stick with me. Same with other movies or TV shows with a lot of fighting.

Because we both understand each other better, we make better choices. By talking through our feelings, we've been able to set rules for our viewing and for our kids' viewing. We are also respectful of each other's opinions. If something is on and the other doesn't approve, we simply have to make eye contact and give a lifted eyebrow. It's a simple signal, but one that says, "Isn't there something else to watch?"

Watch programs that inspire you. Of course, the truth is that not all of our media choices center on controversial stuff. The last two movies I watched were *Charlotte's Web* and *Eragon* with my family. And most of our television watching involves sci-fi, which my family loves, and home decorating programs, which I like.

Recently I was talking to my friend Jennifer about the influence of media, and she made a good point. "Funny, I think at one time people were worried that TV would replace people's interests. Instead, TV has conformed to people's interests. My husband, Paul, can't hunt all year long, but he enjoys watching and learning about the sport all year long," Jennifer said. "I can't travel constantly, but the travel channel can take me places almost any time of day. I love history. Hey, there's a channel for that too." Jennifer also mentioned that she and her husband enjoy ballroom dancing, and because the public's interest has been sparked by shows like *Dancing with the Stars*, their classes are filling up. "TV has brought people back to dancing," Jennifer said. "Is this bad?"

Not in my book.

Understand the effect media has on the spirituality of our world. Yes, we understand TV's truth versus God's truth, but what about the rest of the world? It seems like dozens of new shows every season focus on themes like angels, demons, psychics, and the like. Yet there are other, more subtle influences that may be easy to overlook. Here is one example:

In the fall of 2005, Oprah Winfrey entered her 20th season as the celebrated host of *The Oprah Winfrey Show*. In those two decades, she has amassed over $1.4 billion, assembled a U.S. television audience of more than 49 million viewers each week (not including her broadcasts in 122 other countries), and informed her viewers on matters ranging from genocide in Rwanda to the best-tasting oatmeal cookies.

According to a 2006 article in *USA Today*, however, Oprah's influence entered the spiritual realm at the turn of the century: "By the late '90s, Winfrey's focus was Change Your Life TV, and a New Age message was more prevalent. She preached, making the message of *her* life—take responsibility, and greatness will follow—the substance of the show. Keep a personal journal, purchase self-indulgent gifts, take time for *you* because *you* deserve it. The notes rang true to millions of viewers."

Going even further, Cathleen Falsani, religion writer for the *Chicago Sun-Times*, suggested: "I wonder, has Oprah become America's pastor?" There is evidence to support this theory. A November 2006 poll conducted by Beliefnet .com—a site that looks at how religions and spirituality intersect with popular culture—found that 33 percent of its 6,600 respondents said Winfrey has had "a more profound impact" on their spiritual lives than their clergypersons. Chris Altrock—minister of Highland Street Church of Christ in Memphis, Tennessee—claims: "Our culture is changing as churches are in decline and the bulk of a new generation is growing up outside of religion." Altrock claims that people are turning up at what he calls "The Church of Oprah" instead.[3]

Have you and your husband stopped to consider some of the subtle spiritual messages coming through your TV? If not, it might make for a good talk.

Choose wisely. It is important for John and me to listen to that still, small voice. As Christians, God's Spirit lives within us and is quick to convict us if we heed Him. "Never dull your sense of being your utmost for His highest—your best for His glory," writes Oswald Chambers in *My Utmost for His Highest*. "For you, doing certain things would be craftiness coming into your life for a purpose other than what is the highest and best, and it would dull the motivation that God has given you. Many people have turned back because they are afraid to look at things from God's perspective."[4]

So what is God's perspective on that program you're watching? that movie? that CD you're listening to?

When it comes to media, sometimes you need to remember that the best option is turning it off—especially if you have a gut feeling that is isn't a good choice for you, your marriage, or your faith. Instead, go play a game, talk, or read a book side by side. Don't think about what you're missing out on but about what you gain instead.

MY TAKE ON IT

. . . .

We are really trying to focus on playing games with our kids before we turn on the TV or pop in a DVD. Now that our son is three, this is much easier, because all of us can participate in many games. And I keep a tight rein on what the kids watch because I don't want to have to explain away things they've seen or heard that they now believe must be true because they were on the TV.

—Cara, born in 1974

Indiana, married eleven years

My husband and I tend to be drawn toward similar programs. There have been a few times when I believe a child is capable of watching a certain show and my husband doesn't think it's appropriate—mainly the newer cartoons.

—Lesley, born in 1975

California, married eight years

After the kids go to bed, my husband and I watch the news. We tend to fall asleep on the couch at some point between weather and sports. One of us eventually stumbles off the couch and drags the other up to bed. This nightly ritual leaves little time for communication or heart-to-heart talks, much less marital intimacy.

—Michelle, born in 1971

Ohio, married thirteen years

If you let it, the media can tell you that it's *okay* to give up on your marriage and move on, that no one will be affected by it, and that it's all the other person's fault. The Boomers are the ones running the media at this time, and they are cool with the "it's all about me" way of thinking.

—Chris, born 1976

Michigan, married ten years

Today I was thinking about how the media (especially TV) affects our Gen X marriages. We've heard all the bad stuff, but could there be something good there? Could watching couples on funny sitcoms teach us to laugh at ourselves? Could all those soaps we watched as kids make the dramas in our lives seem smaller and more easily handled? In my marriage (with three young children), our "alone time" is TV time. It is at the very end of the day, when we are both exhausted. We curl up together in front of the TV. We laugh and talk about whatever we're watching. Sometimes we watch a program to be entertained, and sometimes we watch a program that actually teaches us something. I'm not convinced that this is a bad scenario. I recently asked my grandparents what they used to do after the kids were in bed (before TV was around). They played cards, either together or with friends. They laughed and talked about the game as they played. How is this different from my TV scenario? I really don't think it is all that different. (By the way, in true Gen X form, my favorite TV shows are the reality TV shows.)

—Jennifer, born in 1969

Wisconsin, married thirteen years

TV was a big part of growing up. My husband and I still laugh about *The Munsters, Hogan's Heroes, McHale's Navy.* Although we didn't grow up together, we have the same memories of those shows. Those were the TV programs on every afternoon. If you were home sick from school, that's what you watched. I still can't watch *The Munsters* without craving chicken soup or tea and toast! Of course, music was a big influencer as well. I love to watch the "'70s Music Explosion" infomercial because I can sing the words to every song, and I remember what it was like to be a child in the seventies. And, of course, being in high school in the eighties, with music videos and MTV. Our lives revolved around the shade of Madonna's hair on any given day. If it weren't for the music of the eighties, we probably wouldn't have had big hair, Day-Glo clothes, and shoulder pads! How did media define the person I've become? That's a tough one. Well, I think because we have so much more information at our fingertips, my generation is so much more informed than previous generations. We know so much more data—or at least can find answers easily. But I think that's a double-edged sword, because sometimes there's information overload. Too much information makes decision making unnecessarily difficult. In addition, I believe that news in general, and the way things are reported, affects me as well as my generation. As a group, Gen Xers seem to be more scared than previous generations. We hear on the news, in graphic detail, about pretty much every violent thing in our society. Add to that, graphic and violent police and crime dramas, and living a normal life can start to get very scary. For example, we don't let our kids play outside without supervision like our parents did. I don't think the problem is that the world has gotten so much worse as it is that now we know (and can *see*) how bad it is.

—MD, born in 1968

New Jersey, married eleven years

AND ONE MORE THING...

According to *Forbes* magazine, the ten most influential celebrities of 2006 were:

1. Tom Cruise
2. The Rolling Stones
3. Oprah Winfrey
4. U2
5. Tiger Woods
6. Steven Spielberg
7. Howard Stern
8. 50 Cent
9. The cast of The Sopranos
10. Dan Brown

FYI, there are a few Gen Xers in this bunch:

Tom: born 1962

Tiger: born 1975

50 Cent: born 1975

Dan Brown: born 1964

8 SWEET Child o'MINE

Children Redefine "Marriage Partnership"

Where do we go now?

GUNS N' ROSES, APPETITE FOR DESTRUCTION, *1987*, GEFFEN

Children are a welcome addition to families, but their presence unquestionably affects every aspect of married life. In our child-centered society, it is important to focus on God and each other…even with little ones wrapped around our knees. Of course, Cory was already nine months old when John and I got married—we had a ready-made family. Having two more kids in the next three years added to the fun.

Needless to say, we all had some adjusting to do in our first years of marriage. For example, Cory liked to sleep with Mom and didn't want another guy taking his place. On the nights when he found his way into our bed, he'd turn sideways and kick John with all his might. *And who said babies are innocent?*

But this wasn't even our biggest struggle. Rather, it was my belief that I knew best when it came to raising the kids. After all, I was a stay-at-home mom and around the kids all day. How dare John come home from work and have different ideas about how things should run? Let's just say it caused more than one moment of conflict.

"No matter how many children God gives you, it's important to operate jointly in parenting," say Dennis and Barbara Rainey, authors of *Staying Close*. "Again and again, I see families where the woman is expected to raise the kids. Contrary to male expectations, women are not made physically, emotionally, or spiritually to rear children by themselves."[1]

Over time, and after a lot of frustration, I figured out three things: (1) John sometimes knew what he was talking about, (2) I could learn from his ideas, and (3) the kids benefit from a close relationship with their dad.

John was firm but loving. And he was fun. By raising our kids *together*, instead of trying to balance marriage and solo parenting, my life got easier in many ways.

Hmm...maybe that's why God designed children to be raised by both a mother and father?

A Plan and a Purpose

"Marriage is...a *purposeful* relationship. All research indicates that an intimate marriage provides the safest and most productive climate for raising children," writes Gary Chapman in *The Four Seasons of Marriage*.[2] The more time parents spend talking about issues, taking parenting classes, and providing a united front, the more purposeful their parenting. They can come up with a plan and help each other implement it.

Husbands and wives also bring unique input and insight, depending on how they were raised and the type of resources they turn to for advice.

Parents have become better educated about the needs of their children and are being more intentional about their parenting. They are making more sacrifices and working harder at building relationships with their kids than the parents of Xers did, resulting in closer relationships between N-Geners [Next-Gen kids] and their parents.[3]

Of course, joining together as a team is sometimes easier said than done. Dr. John Roseman writes:

> Today's typical wife, as soon as she becomes a parent, begins to act as if she took a marriage vow that read, "I take you to be my husband, until children do us part."
>
> I can remember a time, and not too long ago, when a wife who became a mother remained first and foremost a wife. A woman who worked outside the home was referred to as a "working wife," and a woman who worked in the home was referred to as a "housewife."
>
> But a paradigm shift has occurred in our way of thinking that is reflected in the terms we use to describe a woman's employment status. Today's woman in the same circumstances is referred to as a "working mom" or a "stay-at-home mom." Now, some might think that is an improvement. After all, who wants to be married to her house? But I think the change is more of a reflection of the culture's shift of importance from being a wife to being a mother. Our focus has shifted from a home that is centered on the marriage unit to one that is centered on the children…. This shift came about largely because America's shifted to a self-esteem based child-rearing philosophy, and women became persuaded that the mother who paid the most attention to and did the most for her child was the best mom of them all.[4]

I watch this perception play out in the lives of many women I know. Gen Xers are very focused on their children—sometimes to the point of sacrificing their marriages. And I know firsthand because for many years I placed more emphasis on my role as mom than on my role as wife. My time, energy, devotion went to the kids first, and John got the leftovers.

It wasn't until the kids were in middle school that I realized the best thing I can do for my kids is to love their dad. Their very lives depend upon the strength of our relationship; if it crumbles, their world does too.

Additionally, the way John and I interact serves as our children's model for marriage. In fact, the type of marriage I have with John is most likely the kind my kids will have too. That's huge.

My Take on It

I've been thinking about how our children affect our marriage. They do give us a common "purpose" or maybe "project." Trips to Disneyland are more fun. But I guess the kids also keep us apart. Before kids we worked together and were home together. We did everything together. Now I am at home with the kids while my husband is at work. Then in the evening we are often off meeting the different needs of different kids. We fall into bed physically, emotionally, and spiritually drained. We still go out and do things together, but not without a bit of planning. Before, it was natural to be together just the two of us; now it is a special occasion. I once read a little sign that said, "My children have saved me from self-indulgence." Yet there are times when I would just like to sit and talk with my husband. Is that self-indulgent?

—Jennifer, born in 1969

Wisconsin, married thirteen years

I am the parent who tries to teach my kids how to play well with others, how to respect animals, why cleaning up after yourself is important. I'm in charge of the teeth brushing, the baths, getting dressed—all the daily rituals. My husband is more of the disciplinarian, and he's also the "let's just have fun today" parent. He's the one who plans family outings to the beach and eating junk food. Neither is wrong or right; we just do different stuff with the kids so they have variety, I guess!

—Melissa Ann, born in 1982

California, married five years

Well, getting a shower tops my priority list these days! I think we used to really have "things" at the top of our priority list. Also, we used to think about ourselves a lot. Basically I think we were selfish with our time and our money. We used to talk about the new car or the new house as personal goals in our life. Now we focus on raising Christian children with Christian values above all else. That requires giving of ourselves and our time, and we love doing that! Go figure. Staying home with them definitely changes what things we can buy, and new cars and new houses are just not as important. When I see the wonderful little people my children are turning into, it makes me very happy that I reprioritized my list.

—Kristy, born in 1971

Texas, married fifteen years

Well, of course, the conflict is between the way we think we should parent and the way we actually do. It's very easy to get depressed and imagine that my best is just not good enough. What I often have to remind myself is that God chose my husband and me to be the parents of our daughter, and there are specific things about us that make us the perfect mom and dad for her. That, to me, is really comforting.

—MD, born in 1968

New Jersey, married eleven years

We don't always agree on discipline issues. I tend to be a softie, and my husband is strict. He likes to tell me how to feed, dress, and bathe our son even though he isn't participating in these activities—and that really irritates me! Sometimes I feel like he doesn't trust me to raise our son.

—Stacey, born in 1975

California, married four years

Everybody Wants to Rule the World

Welcome to your life...

TEARS FOR FEARS, SONGS FROM THE BIG CHAIR, 1985, MERCURY

"Nothing ever lasts forever," sang Tears for Fears (remember them?). "Everybody wants to rule the world." The cool thing is that as parents, you do. For a short time, you and your spouse make up your child's entire world, for better or worse.

You've witnessed how our generation was affected by what happened in our world as we grew up. Well, your marriage—you and your spouse working together—will have the same impact on your kids.

There is so much I could talk about when it comes to raising kids...and in fact I did in *Generation NeXt Parenting*. But overall, here is my Top 12 list of the best things a married couple can do *together* for their kids:

1. Spend time working out a philosophy of discipline and child training.
2. Read the Bible together...and let your kids see you do it. Read the Bible to your kids too.
3. Study Christian parenting books.
4. Talk to people whose children you admire.
5. Have daily "couch time" where your kids see the two of you talking about your day. It will give them security to see their parents communicate. They will know all is well in their world.
6. Never disagree about discipline in front of the children. Children know how to play one parent against the other.
7. Be loyal to one another and stand by each other, even when you don't think the other person has handled the situation correctly. It's better to work it out afterward, in private.
8. Let loose once in a while. Life doesn't always have to be serious.
9. Pray together as a family.

10. Love one another, and show your loyalty to each other.

11. Let the kids see you handle disagreements and resolutions respectfully.

12. Trust that God chose you and your spouse specifically for this job. He placed you together in this time in history, with these kids, for a reason.

MY TAKE ON IT

To be an ideal Christian parent, one must teach the gospel to their children as well as set a good example. I fail to be the ideal Christian parent, but I'm learning to do better each day. Anyone can love their children and provide all the materialistic things they need. But teaching your children about the love of the Lord is one of the most meaningful gifts they can ever receive.

—Lesley, born in 1979

California, married eight years

My children have given me an ever-present reason to work through the tough times with my husband. I don't want to leave them with the painful legacy of divorce or to be like parents who are married in name only (as I experienced). Our children have brought so much joy and laughter into our home and have helped my husband and me to see how vital understanding our growing up is so that we can leave a good legacy of love to our kids.

—Amy, born in 1970

Georgia, married twelve years

Having kids helps us deal with the things we learned from our parents—things we want to change for the better. Kids will also expose the areas we thought we could hide and not deal with, our own shortcomings.

—Chris, born in 1976

Michigan, married ten years

AND ONE MORE THING...

BOOMERS grew up in an era when traditional family values were still cherished by adults.

GEN XERS grew up in the shadow of their rebellious parents and were more likely to experience an unconventional lifestyle.

BOOMERS felt that they were special people, entitling them to the best the world had to offer.

GEN XERS feel as if they've been forgotten, if not intentionally limited. They would like to have the best, but they realistically maintain lower expectations.

BOOMERS grew up accepting the possibility of change but balanced it with a desire for stability.

GEN XERS have grown up knowing only change. They desire to have influence over the changes around them.

BOOMERS matured in a period when information was highly valued but a difficult commodity to obtain.

GEN XERS have grown up during the information explosion.

BOOMERS were rebellious, but they remained convinced of the value of education.

GEN XERS view education as a necessity to be tolerated.

BOOMERS have seen work as an end to itself. A significant portion of their identity comes from their status and performance on the job.

GEN XERS view work as a means to an end. They are not as willing to work long hours to climb the corporate ladder.

BOOMERS have experienced unparalleled economic growth in their lifetimes.

GEN XERS expect the economy to stabilize or decline in comparison with their parents' experience.

BOOMERS have remained an abundantly self-indulgent, bold, and agressive lot.

GEN XERS have always felt inferior. Although oftentimes selfish and unyielding on principles, their principles are different.

BOOMERS valued relationships but built them in new ways. They were the original networkers, a concept that fit well with their utilitarian view of life and people.

GEN XERS have outright rejected the impersonal, short-term, fluid relational character of their parents.[5]

9

DIRTY Laundry

Everyday Stuff of Life

Well, I coulda been an actor, but I wound up here…

DON HENLEY, I CAN'T STAND STILL, 1982, GEFFEN

marriage isn't all romance or heart connections. Don't we wish! No, the everyday stuff of life includes housework, yard work, and more. Much more.

Like the time I served John a bowlful of stew I'd left simmering all day in our new Crock-Pot. We'd been married for only a few weeks, and I wanted to embrace the role of domestic goddess. I knew I was no June Cleaver—or even Alice from *The Brady Bunch* for that matter. Still, wanting to do this marriage thing right, I purchased a cookbook and set to work.

I'll never forget the look on my new husband's face as he took a big bite of beef stew, chewed slowly, and swallowed. "Uh, honey," he asked delicately, "was that a grape?"

"A grape?" I pushed my spoon around in the bowl, my smile fading. Sure enough, the raisins (which the recipe *called* for, by the way) had swelled into big, plump grapes. Not only that, the grapes had given the whole pot a decidedly "fruity" flavor. Even after picking every last one out, we were forced to deem the meal inedible.

My new husband was kind as I blubbered on about never having made stew before. In fact, as he soon found out, I'd never made much of anything. Growing up in the recession of the eighties, with both of my parents working, nightly meals generally consisted of TV dinners or Banquet fried chicken from a box. When my mom did cook from scratch, I was usually at cheerleading practice or studying for a test. Besides, it was easier for Mom to do it herself than show me how.

After that first "grape stew" dinner (and a dozen similar ones to follow), my enthusiasm for domesticity waned. How in the world was I going to get the hang of this wife thing? Where was Caroline Ingalls when I needed her? *Ma, help!*

A hundred years ago, women trained their daughters in the fine art of caring for a home. When a new bride stepped into her role as wife, she was prepared for her domestic duties—sewing, cleaning, and yes, cooking.

I entered marriage with good intentions but very little training. Still, I was a smart girl. I made the dean's list in college, for heaven's sake. How hard could it be?

With practice, I learned to cook and clean…but that didn't mean I liked it. Remember those expectations I talked about in chapter 1? I wanted John to do *more* around the house. *Anything would be an improvement,* I thought. I tried complaining. I tried nagging. I made a wonderful martyr.

Then I decided to pray about it. To my astonishment, instead of zapping my husband, God took me back to my unfulfilled expectations. In His gentle way, He asked me to look at my heart. He reminded me of the passage in the gospel of John where Jesus washed His disciples' feet. Jesus knew that the Father had put all things under His power and that He had come from God and was returning to God, so He got up from the meal, removed His outer clothing, and wrapped a towel around His waist. Then He poured water into a basin and began washing His disciples' feet, drying them with the towel.

Now that I, your Lord and Teacher, have washed your feet, you also should wash one another's feet. I have set you an example that you should do as I have done for you. I tell you the truth, no servant is greater than his master, nor is a messenger greater than the one who sent him. Now that you know these things, you will be blessed if you do them. (John 13:14–17)

Jesus didn't serve the disciples because He was inferior. He served out of power. Out of love.

"We can all see God in exceptional things, but it requires the growth of spiritual discipline to see God in every detail," Oswald Chambers wrote. "Never believe that the so-called random events of life are anything less than God's appointed order. Be ready to discover His divine designs anywhere and everywhere."[1]

Really? Could God's divine designs be found in the ordinary stuff of life too?

There are two ways we can approach the household duties—with resentment and competition ("I do more than he/she does") or with a heart of service and love, as Jesus showed us. The latter is the wiser course.

My Take on It

My husband's mom is the traditional farm wife. She still makes lunch and dinner for my father-in-law every day, even though she works outside the home. He won't fix himself something to eat even if she doesn't get home until 9 p.m.! My husband, on the other hand, will unload the dishwasher, throw a load of a laundry in, or pick up some playthings without even being asked when he sees I'm getting behind. He is glad to vacuum, make a meal, or do some other chore if I ask him to. I'm not sure his dad would lift a finger even when asked. For him, working on the farm is enough.

—Jessica, born in 1975
Iowa, married four years

Some days I want to just lie in bed all day and read a good book. And then I think of the chain e-mail I got a few years ago: "...The man comes home from work and his children are in their underwear playing in the mud in the front yard.

Concerned, he goes into the house and sees that the furniture is out of place, the fridge is open wide, half-eaten food is scattered, the house is in general disarray. He runs upstairs, hears the water on in the bathroom and sees another child playing in the flood on the bathroom floor. He picks up speed and opens his bedroom door and sees his wife still in her pj's reading a book. He asks her what happened. She replies, 'You know how every day you come home from work and ask what on earth I did today? Well, today I didn't do it.'" I wish I were brave enough to try that!

—Melissa Ann, born in 1982

California, married five years

My husband came from a very traditional home—my mother-in-law has a master's in home economics from an Ivy League college. Talk about intimidating! She has always stayed home. I can't compete with Betty Crocker, and I really don't want to either. I'm not cut from that cloth. But it has created tension in our marriage because I feel my husband is trying to stuff me into his mother's mold or compares me and finds me lacking—often subconsciously. And I know I'm not Betty Crocker, especially when I'm working. It's very frustrating to feel that all of the household responsibilities fall on my shoulders when we've both worked all day.

—Cara, born in 1974

Indiana, married eleven years

Another One Bites the Dust

Are you ready, are you ready for this...

QUEEN, THE GAME, 1980, EMI/ELEKTRA

Through the years, I've tried out many home organization, cleaning, and care systems. But I've devised a system that works even better:

1. I thank God for my role.

"Without question, the very idea of roles is negative for some people today, especially for some women," write Robert Lewis and William Hendricks, authors of *Rocking the Roles*.

> They see roles as confining. Roles put people in a box. Roles limit choices. Roles keep women "in their place." Any talk of roles brings ugly images of abuse that women have had to endure. The whole notion of roles has become suspect as a backward, chauvinistic way of looking at relationships.
>
> Well, that's not what I mean by roles.... When I speak of a role, I mean *the essential function* that God has designed a man or a woman to fulfill in a marriage relationship. Let me add that while those roles differ, that does not mean that one is superior and one is inferior. Both are of equal value and importance. ... As far as Scripture is concerned, roles address one's responsibility, not one's rank.[2]

This makes me think of something a friend once said to me: "God cursed Eve by giving her pain in childbirth. God cursed Adam by telling him he had to make a living from the earth by the sweat of his brow. Eve must not have thought her curse was bad enough because she took on Adam's too."

God created men with an innate desire to provide and protect and women with an inner desire to comfort and care. I'm not saying that women shouldn't work outside the home or that men can't stay home and care for a house and family. But I personally find fulfillment in seeing my family enjoy a nice dinner or gazing at a shiny kitchen (for the whole two seconds it stays clean).

Besides, does the lack of roles really work? "Despite twenty or more years of positive press and experimentation with the model of the 'role-less marriage,' couples don't appear any closer to achieving 'equality' in their relationships than before. Instead, I find a lot of confusion, heartbreak, frustration, and denial," wrote Arlie Hochschild in *The Second Shift: Working Parents and the Revolution at Home*.

In the role-less marriage, you'd expect [household chores] to be split fifty-fifty. Yet twenty-five years of research on who does the chores shows that employed married women work roughly fifteen hours longer each week than men. Over a year, they [work] an extra month of twenty-four-hour days a year. Over a dozen years, it [is] an extra year of twenty-four-hour days. Most women without children spend much more time than men on housework; with children, they devote more time to both housework and childcare.[3]

Why push, fight, and scream for something that doesn't fit who God designed us to be?

"While the rest of the world runs after grandiose and unattainable ideals, married partners walk the humbler but more accessible path of simple caring for one another from one day to the next. It is a task that is not very glorious from the point of view of the world, but one which could hardly be more important in the eyes of God," writes Mike Mason in *The Mystery of Marriage*.[4]

I agree.

2. I ask for help.

There is something very crucial I've learned recently. Ready?

John cannot *read my mind*.

What a concept!

I remember days spent cleaning the house, cooking, answering the phone, and stewing (in my emotions, not my Crock-Pot). Why? Because amid my mad scramble, John would walk in, give me a kiss, and immediately head to the back room to hang out with the kids in front of the TV.

At dinnertime, when my eyes brimmed over with tears, he would ask, "Honey, what's wrong?"

"You should know what's wrong!" I would fume.

But of course he didn't.

"Countless studies prove that unrealized or unfulfilled expectations contribute to a big chunk of marriage dissatisfaction," says Toni Poynter, author of *Now and Forever: Advice for a Strong Marriage*. "And the problem is, when you stop talking, these expectations remain unknown or unspoken. We should be earning a PhD in our spouses, but too often we drop that difficult course of study and fall back on what we think our spouse ought to be like."[5]

One night John and I talked about my anger over unmet expectations. I told him how much I appreciate when he helps me out—that stepping in, asking where I need assistance, and then pitching in are better than bringing me six dozen roses. Seriously.

John had no idea I felt this way because I had never verbalized my frustration in a rational way. After I learned that whining and nagging didn't work, I had switched to playing the martyr. But once I respectfully voiced my feelings, John began to ask how he could help. He did this out of love. And he soon discovered that a happy wife is a joy to be around.

I realized through that experience I don't have to do everything. I also needed to ask instead of throwing myself a pity party.

3. I focus on family.

It has been said, "What you spend your days doing will determine what you spend your lifetime doing." There's a lot of truth in that. Five years from now, I don't want to look back and regret not spending enough time with my husband, children, and friends.

"Pay attention to the messages you're sending your family," writes Denece Scho-field, author of *Confessions of a Happily Organized Family*. "Don't ever give them the impression the house is more important than they are. Somewhere along the line we've come to the conclusion that the house has to be cleaner and tidier for people who *don't* live there."[6]

Will life really fall apart if I leave the dishes in the sink overnight? (No. I've tested it.) I don't want to pass up making a memory to clean a kitchen that will be dirty again tomorrow. I've also learned not to stress when someone is coming over. So what if everything isn't perfect if perfection means a cranky, frantic spouse?

4. I make a plan and stick to it.

Not having a plan equals setting myself up for failure. And who wants to do that?

"One of the biggest problems with housework is that it's never done. You can work for hours and hours and never feel like you've accomplished anything," adds Schofield. "But a schedule eliminates those feelings of frustration by giving you a stopping point. The work may not be finished, but *you* are. Monday's work can be completed. Tuesday's work can be done—and so on. Sure, there may be other areas that need your attention, but that's scheduled for another day."[7]

5. I remember that rigid people are brittle and break easily.

I try to be flexible about my expectations. I also try not to fret over little things, especially when they don't meet my standards. A lot of women cut their own throats by having too high a standard. If you want your spouse to help you, you must affirm his efforts—even if those efforts are not what you consider perfect.

6. I turn to God when I feel discontent and unsatisfied.

Can I glorify God by serving my spouse? I believe the answer is yes. My expectations about earthly comforts will never be met, but maybe my love and service will cause someone to take notice—especially the one I vowed to love and cherish for life.

"In a man-centered view, we will maintain our marriage as long as our earthly comforts, desires, and expectations are met," writes Gary Thomas, author of *Sacred Marriage*. "In a God-centered view, we preserve our marriage because it brings glory to God and points a sinful world to a reconciling Creator."[8]

My Take on It

I do all the laundry, all the cooking, all the cleaning, and really everything that goes along with running the household. If I complain, my husband reminds me that I have three little assistants and maybe I should utilize them more efficiently. As the kids are getting older, they are helping more and more, and my job is getting easier and easier. There was never a question in my mind that I wanted to be home if we had children. My husband, on the other hand, wanted me to do it all. He wanted me to do all the housework, raise the children, and hold down a job. I know some women are able to do this, but not me. I believe that I am blessed to be at home. I think of the Titus 2 women and the woman from Proverbs 31—I want to be like them. Sometimes I do get impatient and demand that he at least pick up after himself, but most of the time I find joy in making his life easier, better. After all, he is the one getting up at 5 a.m.

—Jennifer, born in 1969

Wisconsin, married thirteen years

My husband and I actually make a list of all of the chores around the house; then we divide them between the two of us based on how much time each one takes. We take turns choosing and then type up the list and keep it in our office. For us that alleviated the fights about who did what chore last and whose turn it was to do it this time.

—Dana, born 1980

California, married three-and-a-half years

My grandmother would have never asked Grandpa to help with the cooking or cleaning. He probably didn't even know how. It was her responsibility. He brought home the paycheck, and she took care of the household and children. In recent years, women have been working outside the home more than ever before. Necessity has caused husbands to step in and help more with the housework and child rearing than ever before.

—Michelle, born in 1971

Ohio, married thirteen years

I am a total Type A personality, with ambition on overdrive (until I had kids). I had to be the best at everything. My mom and stepmom were both strong women (by that, I mean women who asserted their opinions and resisted their husbands with explosive results). By four-and-a-half years in, I realized my marriage was falling apart. I was pregnant with my second. We were both church attendees who prayed, but we were all about religion (and with it judgment) rather than relationship (and with it love). I started reading two books: *Making Your Husband Feel Loved* and *Romancing Your Husband*. After this, through love, I *chose* to do things around the house rather than just "clean up this pigsty." I did what I knew would make my husband more relaxed and happy at home, and he did the same for me. I stopped feeling guilty that I wasn't superwoman, with a perfectly clean house, well-groomed children, etc. We have really sought to serve each other in love, and our roles have naturally sifted down from that. I praise God that the longer we're married, the less we disagree and the more we become one. That is the opposite of what I've seen so many others do.

—Tiffany, born in 1976

Michigan, married ten years

And One More Thing...

How could I have known that one of the most profound lessons I would learn about love would come from eavesdropping on a conversation between my camp counselor and one of the high-school students in our cabin? The message earlier that evening from the head counselor had been about sex. The gist of it, as I recall, was that sex was not an evil that marriage permitted, but rather a gift that marriage protected. That sounds good now. But we mostly interpreted it as further efforts on the part of the staff to discourage any questionable activities between the boys and girls at the camp.

But one of the guys in the cabin was a little disturbed. I heard him address our counselor with a slight challenge in his voice: "Well, John, it's a little late for me to hear that message."

"Why is that?"

"Well, Sharon and I have already…you know…"

"'You know,' what?" the counselor asked.

"We, uh, you know—went all the way," the student said, speeding up his words at the end but expressing himself with a hint of pride.

"What do you mean, 'all the way'?" John pressed, drawing out the last phrase as if to make up for the speed with which it had been uttered. I couldn't believe the counselor was so dense. *What was he thinking?*

"You know, *all the way,*" the boy stressed, as if saying it with emphasis would clarify the meaning.

But the counselor didn't let him off the hook. "No, I don't know what you mean. What are you talking about?"

"You know, we had sex!" he blurted out, exasperated.

"Ohhhhh, *that's* what you mean," John said with a show of surprise. "And you think that's going all the way?"

"Well, yes."

"That's not going all the way at all," he explained. "I'll tell you what going all the way is. There's a guy in my neighborhood who has five kids, and his wife is now in a wheelchair. He gets the kids off to school each morning, sells insurance all day to make a living, then comes home and makes dinner for the family. And at the end of the evening, he looks his wife in the eye and tells her he loves her. I know he means it, too, because he tells me he's the luckiest guy he knows to have been blessed with her. *That's* what going all the way is."[9]

My Take on It

True romance is going to sleep together every night and waking up together every morning. True romance is running out at 11 p.m. to buy cough syrup and orange juice when your spouse is sick. True romance is saying, "Thanks for making dinner, it was really good"—even when it wasn't. True romance is long-term. It's saying, "I love you"—even when he leaves his dirty socks in the middle of the floor…again. It's him saying, "You're beautiful," even as you find a new wrinkle or gray hair or when you didn't have time to do your hair and makeup today because the kids were sick.

—Michelle, born in 1968

New Jersey, married eleven years

10
HANDS^{to}HEAVEN

Church Service

So raise your hands to heaven and pray.

BREATHE, ALL THAT JAZZ, 1987, A&M

while I was researching the subject of church service and its connection to marriage, I had a difficult time finding quotable material in other books. A few mentioned how attending church was important but didn't elaborate on the reason. And there was very little mention of the struggles many married couples have with church leaders, fellow church members, or the church itself.

On the other hand, my Gen X friends were extremely vocal about their feelings, opinions, and beliefs concerning church. When I sent out my questionnaire, an abundance of responses poured in. Maybe Gen Xers are the only ones stepping back and saying, "Wait a minute here…"?

It would seem that many Gen Xers have been deeply impacted by the church. So instead of "My Take on It" in this chapter, you'll find excerpts from Gen Xers sprinkled liberally throughout the following pages. And within these quotes, wisdom abounds! But first, let me share my story…

Growing up in the 1970s and '80s was a tough time to consider having a relationship with God. It's not that God did anything wrong, but His servants sure had a rough go of it.

On March 19, 1987, Jim Bakker resigned from his ministry. His resignation was prompted by disclosure of a December 6, 1980, extramarital affair with Jessica Hahn, his secretary. In the wake of this sudden publicity, a grand jury found evidence that Bakker had skimmed millions of dollars donated by his followers. On December 5, 1988, Bakker was indicted. He was convicted of conspiracy and fraud in early 1989. He was sentenced to forty-five years in prison, but his sentence was later commuted.

Jim Bakker wasn't the only public figure facing moral problems. It seemed like every month another political figure or spiritual leader's conduct was exposed in the media.

> Political and environmental issues and events left these young people with the sense that the adults were ruining their futures, giving them a sense of hopelessness and cynicism. Moral failures of public figures, including parents, convinced them that people, especially older ones in established institutions, could probably not be trusted. Many of the children of the eighties have an ingrained skepticism about life.[1]

These things tainted my view of religious leaders while I was growing up. But when John and I married, we made church a vital part of our lives. We were there Sunday morning, Sunday night, and Wednesday night. Unfortunately, the same moral failings that we witnessed with Jim Bakker struck close to home…not once, but twice. Both situations involved close friends and church leaders we respected, and they threw us into a tailspin.

John and I continued to attend church, but we now realized two things: (1) Anyone could be tempted and fall into sin and (2) humans weren't made to be put on pedestals; when they are, the fall is a hard one.

We also evaluated our own opinions of church. In the process, we discovered that pastors weren't meant to do all the work for the body of Christ (something many people believed and lived out in our growing-up years). The word *church* actually means "called-out assembly." It's vital for each member of the body of Christ to roll up their sleeves and serve.

God tested this last theory when He led us to our current church.

We had been in Montana for only a year when we realized that something was missing. We were part of a fantastic church, but we interacted only on the fringes. For example, we had volunteered to serve in different capacities but were told our help wasn't needed. Whoever heard of volunteers for children's church being turned away?

Around the same time, we heard from friends who attended a different congregation. It was a small church, and a lot more traditional than we were used to. But through a series of specific events, we knew God was calling us to attend their church.

I'll admit, I cried my eyes out during the first service. I loved the bigger, more exciting services at our former church. Yet I realized that God knew best, and I trusted Him—even as I pouted over what I was missing.

A month later, Pastor Daniel and his wife visited our home. They heard our testimonies and asked what areas we felt God was leading us to serve in. It was then that John shared about the dramatic children's church ministry God had laid on our hearts.

After listening to John's ideas, Pastor Daniel's lips curled into a smile. "I've been praying for something like this for two years," he said, then told us about another couple in the congregation with the same passion. That couple just happened to be the friends who had invited us to the church. We had no idea of their desire, nor they of ours. But once we got together with them, our children's church was born. We've been faithfully serving every week for the last ten years. And we love it!

Around that time, something else started happening that made us realize God was clearly at work. Thanks in part to our growing children's ministry, the church pews began filling with young families, many of whom had never before been part of a church body. We started with twenty children, then watched as the number grew to forty, then sixty, then eighty. In the last year, we have had over *seven hundred church attendees* each Sunday, 120 of them kids ages four through nine who attend our children's church program.

Through this, God has shown me one thing: He didn't send us to what I'd consider "the perfect church." Instead, He called us to serve *for His glory* in a place that has become home for us and for hundreds of others.

What About the Rest of Us?

Even though many Gen Xers are founding their lives and their homes on a relationship with Christ, church attendance is still low within our age group. However, it is rising. According to 2003 statistics by George Barna:

> Over the past century, sociologists have noted that when young adults enter a new life stage—such as...marriage or parenthood—religious faith often becomes a more central and stabilizing factor in their lives. That pattern is evident among the Baby Busters, the country's second-largest generation ever, born between 1965 and 1983. Often described as pessimistic, self-centered, and brooding, the generation is now becoming more family-oriented (more than twice as many Busters are married today as was true just ten years ago, and millions more have children today than a decade earlier), producing a slow but growing acceptance of more traditional Christian activity. Among the changes seen in the Busters is a seven percentage point increase in Sunday school attendance since 1996; a six-point rise in church volunteerism since 1998; a four-point increase in church attendance; a six-point jump in participation in small groups that meet during the week for Bible study, prayer, and fellowship; and a seven-point hike in Bible reading.[2]

Gen Xers are starting to figure out that God designed church to be the body of Christ. A connection with a community of believers is just one of the benefits. They're also discovering that what couples *receive* from a church service isn't nearly as important as what couples can *give* through service.

I can't express the joy that comes with serving in a local church. When I talk with other Gen Xers, we recognize that many of us believe we are part of God's plan for a generation. We are passionate about living out our faith, volunteering in a capacity that matters, uniting with other believers, and building a "family" of like-minded people within (and beyond) the four walls of church.

Gen X Thoughts About Church Service:

◎ **Gen Xers want to attend church but oftentimes don't for various reasons.**

> I suppose waking up for church on Sunday mornings is the biggest conflict my husband and I have. I love when the children go to Sunday school, but more often than not I am unwilling to get myself up and go.
>
> **—Lesley, born in 1979**
>
> **California, married eight years**

◎ **Gen Xers love to serve. They also feel it's important to get their children involved in service.**

> Serving in the church drives home the fact that we are part of a larger spiritual family. It's wonderful for kids to watch their parents use their gifts to serve the church and then grow to a point where they discover ways to serve themselves.
>
> **—Jeanette, born in 1967**
>
> **Nevada, married eighteen years**

> I love to serve. I am constantly amazed at how God will take something I've said or done and use it to make an impact on someone else's life. And I am so grateful for the times when He allows me to see that impact. I worship not because of what God will do for me but because of what He has already done. He alone is worthy of my praise. But out of that, He changes and tweaks me, making me into a woman He can use. Plus, I just have a hard time being served, so it's more natural for me to find slots to serve others.
>
> **—Cara, born in 1974**
>
> **Indiana, married eleven years**

◎ **Gen Xers feel grounded at church. In fact, it oftentimes becomes the extended family they always wished they'd had.**

Right after we were married I wanted to attend church. To me, that meant I had really made it; I was an adult. Looking back, I realize I was "playing house," thinking I was so grown up. Yet church gradually became an important part of our marriage. Church grounds us and our family. It keeps us from flying off in every direction. By attending church together, we are developing a common worldview, common values, and common beliefs. Church is a great place for all of us to meet friends. Our family has connected with other families who also share common values and beliefs. Our church family gives us somewhere to turn when there is a hardship. It also gives us the opportunity to help others in their time of need. And when our kids ask tough questions, church is a great place to find answers. As we grow in our faith at church, and in Bible study, we are growing together and not apart.

—Jennifer, born in 1969

Wisconsin, married thirteen years

◎ **Gen Xers connect with God at church.**

I have to go to church. By that, I don't mean I'll go straight to hell if I don't; I mean every time I'm there God meets me, speaks to me, strengthens me, and gives me the ability to move forward. My not going would be like never seeing my husband, talking to him, kissing him, etc. I honestly don't know how people accomplish *anything* in life without God. I wouldn't want to try.

—Tiffany, born in 1976

Michigan, married ten years

◎ **Gen Xers know their weaknesses, and they look to church to support them in times of need.**

Too many Boomer parents didn't make church a priority and train their children that church attendance is an important part of being a Christian. But it's not about attendance for the sake of attendance. At church I'm challenged by the pastor to learn more and believe more about God. At church I get to worship corporately with the body, and that's a different experience from me alone in my car. And at church I build relationships with other believers so that they have the right and ability to hold me accountable. I also have a group of people that I can call on when I need prayer or support. Lone Ranger Christians are so much easier to pick off because they are weak and isolated.

—Cara, born in 1974

Indiana, married eleven years

Reasons Gen Xers Struggle with Church:

◎ **Gen Xers believe in relationship, not "religion."**

Many churches don't let God move. They try to *control* God, and what they do is create a religion rather than a relationship. People want to open their bulletin and know that it will be a fifty-eight-minute service and that there will be two hymns, two Scripture readings, and a seventeen-minute message. Bye-bye, go home. Xers don't have time for that mess. They are like me. They want to go where God is living, breathing, real, and *welcomed!* They don't want formula religion. They want to know there is something real, bigger than them. Another struggle we have is with hypocrisy. Many Xers watched Mom and Dad party Friday night, wake up with some strange person in their bed Saturday morning, then dress up in their Sunday best. They've seen scandals rock churches and priests abusing kids. They figure if those church people are just like their parents, then why bother? I refute the notion that Xers aren't looking for God. They want a God of power, so they mistakenly turn to other false gods. But in my church I see the Xers, and the generation following them, growing. They come in and see guitars, drums, and singers who are singing, "I will praise You in this storm." And they see real answers. God pricks their hearts, and they drop to their knees at an altar and say, "God, help me in this storm."

—Tiffany, born in 1976

Michigan, married ten years

◎ **Gen Xers have grown up learning to be tolerant of others in all issues except faith.**

Another problem we have is a growing acceptance for other religions. We think, *Two-thirds of the world believes differently than us, and it's too sad to think that they will all go to hell.* So instead we search for intelligence/science that contradicts faith. This could all very well be an excuse for avoiding accountability.

—Angela, born in 1977

Idaho, married seven years

◎ **The authors of *Boomers, Xers, and Other Strangers* agree. They write:**

Growing up in a society that emphasized the rights of various minority groups, [Gen Xers] tend to be more tolerant and accepting of individuals of various backgrounds and lifestyles. Their exposure to so many different beliefs and philosophies, plus their commitment to tolerance, has made it difficult for them to believe that there are any absolute truths in life to live by.[3]

◎ **Gen Xers don't want a list of dos and don'ts; they want to connect with Christ.**

I really hate the masks and the idea that life is fine on Sundays, when Monday through Saturday it isn't. I also get tired of sermons and teaching that hammers on what we "have to do" instead of on how we can grow in our relationship with Christ and listen to the Holy Spirit. All the laws in the world, no matter how achievable they sound, won't help us walk intimately with God.

—Amy, born in 1970

Georgia, married twelve years

◎ **Gen Xers don't want to feel guilty. Instead, they long to be accepted.**

I run away from church when I'm made to feel guilty about not attending as often as I should (or as often as "they" think I should). I run away when I am pushed into attending activities or volunteering for something. I don't like to be pushed. I like to feel welcomed and accepted for just being there. I run toward church when members are welcoming and just accept me. No pushing or guilt trips.

—Lesley, born in 1979

California, married eight years

◎ **Gen Xers have been hurt by church leaders and members in the past. They are a cautious bunch.**

When I was little, my parents divorced. At that time, the priest asked my mom not to take communion because she had sinned by getting divorced. Eventually, they asked her to leave because her ex-husband was having affairs with church members. Rather than support her in this difficult time of life, they blamed her for her ex-husband's issues. This experience led me away from church for a long time. Even after finding a loving church home, I worry that we are not acting right at church and will be reprimanded somehow.

—Michelle, born in 1971

Ohio, married thirteen years

◎ **Gen Xers see the shortfalls of the church.**

At times, churches tend to "eat their own," abusing and overextending those who are always involved because these members can't say no. It's taken many years for my wife and me to both feel comfortable saying no. Yet we have to when we feel that the church/home/work/self balance is off.

—Chris, born in 1974

Florida, married thirteen years

Why Is Church Important?

Despite the many challenges, Gen Xers find joy in growing closer to God and in connecting with a community of believers through church service. Are you involved in serving in a local church body?

Gen Xers need community.

"Another very significant attribute of the Gen Xers is their commitment to people and personal relationship," write Dr. Rick and Kathy Hicks. "They grew up in a time when strong significant relationships were few and far between. Now, as adults, they see the importance of those relationships and will sacrifice many things to nurture them. They may not show much loyalty to the company they work for, but they tend to be very loyal to individual coworkers, friends, and family, through thick and thin."[4]

May I add to that "loyal to fellow church members" too? John and I have friends whom we've attended church with for eleven years. I have others in California whom we attended church with when John and I first got married. They are dear friends. And I'm talking about believers of all ages and backgrounds. In my opinion, it's a small glimpse of what heaven will be like.

Church fosters accountability.

Jen Abbas, author of *Generation Ex*, shares the following story. Though I don't personally know the couple she speaks of, I have friends who have gone down the same path. It's sad to witness. Divorce has become all too common for Christians who walk away from church for various reasons. Perhaps you've seen this sad story played out too:

Both my husband and I came from broken homes. We dated for four years before getting married. We took our faith as seriously as our desire to avoid divorce. We started off so strong and so intentionally. We were involved in Bible study, we read relationship books together, we served in our church together. We were the couple that everyone looked to as a model.

But after the kids came and time went on, we relaxed our efforts, and I think, in hindsight, took our marriage for granted. At least I did once I realized I had been married longer than my mom. Because of my husband's job, we moved around a lot. After a while, we stopped making church attendance a priority. Without a focused commitment to God—something above ourselves—we reverted to looking out for our needs first. We became dissatisfied and instead of talking about it, we let it fester.

He became a workaholic, and I found solace in the arms of his best friend. It's been seven years since our divorce, and I wish I could just go back. I'm so ashamed of what I did. And worse, we both became what we tried so hard to overcome. I am a single mom, just like my mom. He is the estranged dad, just like his father.[5]

Just because you attend church or serve at church, it doesn't mean you don't have to work on your marriage.
"Although our faith gives us access to the skills and commitment needed to make a marriage successful, don't make the mistake of thinking that God is some sort of genie who will protect you from the normal struggles and realities of married life," writes Jen Abbas[6]

Church attendance is one way to connect with God's body. It's also a wonderful opportunity for husbands and wives to serve together. Yet service in church should never take the place of total commitment to your spouse. Service and activity should never make you feel safe from outside temptations.

John and I have watched church leaders fall. We've witnessed our own friends walking away from church and God. We're disheartened by this statistic from George Barna: "Among married born again Christians, 35% have experienced a divorce. That figure is identical to the outcome among married adults who are not born again: 35%."[7]

It's up to us to make a change…by starting in our own home first.

AND ONE MORE THING...

STYLE OF WORSHIP

Gls: Formulaic. Attracted to religious events that are rich with pomp and ornate ceremony.

    Silents: Quiet, reverential. "Be still and know that I am God" approach.

        Boomers: "It's a big message, so spread it in a big way." Slick, professional.

            Xers: Intimate, nonjudgmental, personally connect with "my God."

                Millennials: Eager to integrate all the spiritual threads of their lives. Desire to explore other religious traditions.[8]

ATTITUDE ABOUT GOD

Gls: God is distant and aloof.

    Silents: God is distant but approachable.

        Boomers: God is familiar—we can feel His power working through us.

            Xers: God is a friend, guide, companion, and healer.

                Millennials: God is the nation builder, provider, and protector.[9]

11

LET MY Love Open THE DOOR

Romancing Your Spouse

...to your heart.

PETE TOWNSEND, EMPTY GLASS, 1980, ATLANTIC

I can still remember the night John proposed. We'd asked my mom to babysit my son Cory, and then John drove me to a restaurant seventy miles away for a nice dinner. After that, we walked to a local park and strolled together in the moonlight. We laughed, talked, and joked. John even did a little song and dance, to my delight. Then he led me toward the light of a streetlamp, got down on one knee, produced a beautiful ring, and asked me to marry him.

Even though we live a thousand miles away now, we've been back to visit that park. A huge bridge crossing the Sacramento River has been erected at the very spot he proposed. As we gazed at it, once again in the moonlight, John whispered in my ear, "It's only right that such a beautiful structure be constructed as a monument of our love."

The longer I've been married, the more my idea of romance has changed. Sure, I still enjoy dinner out and walks in the park, but my face really lights up when John sees me in the kitchen and helps me with dinner, or when he picks up the bottle of Mr. Clean and spends forty-five minutes on a Saturday morning making our bathroom shine. Those things mean a lot to me because John sees my need and strives to alleviate some of the work that comes with raising kids, writing books, and serving in church.

Likewise, John appreciates it when I curl up next to him on the couch during a movie…especially one I wouldn't otherwise choose to watch. Or if I make him a sandwich while he's working in the garage. Or give him a massage after a long day at work.

Romance doesn't have to fade away with the years. With or without kids, romance can flame, spread, and provide a warming fire in the hearts of mates.

Romance doesn't have to be trite. True romance impacts the deepest part of our hearts—the place where media, movies, and love songs can't possibly reach.

Addicted to Love

Might as well face it…

ROBERT PALMER, RIPTIDE, 1985, ISLAND RECORDS

As Robert Palmer sang, "Might as well face it, you're addicted to love." Sometimes we look to the wrong places to feed our addiction; it's something we learned during our growing-up years in the 1970s and '80s. Before we talk about ways to romance your spouse, let's examine a few things *not* to do.

Myron A. Marty writes:

> Soap operas attracted 20 million viewers daily, and not just bored housewives and shut-ins. College students were among those hooked on the daily dramas featuring troubled characters in life's continuing crises. As in their earlier days on radio, soaps were typically sponsored by manufacturers of household products.

In 1976, television networks carried fourteen daytime soap operas, totaling forty-five hours each week. Those who missed episodes could learn what happened by reading plot summaries in the *Daytime Serials Newsletter*. The shooting of J.R. Ewing in the 1979–1980 season [cliffhanger of the] prime-time soap opera *Dallas* prompted summer-long speculation on "Who shot J.R.?" An audience of about 83 million tuned in to the show in November 1980, when the culprit was revealed.[1]

So what is true romance?

True romance is lived out, not simply dreamed about. Years ago I loved reading secular romance novels. The men in those books said all the right things at exactly the right moments. They proved their love in extraordinary ways, the chemistry was hot, and they made my heart soar.

One day, while discussing these books with John, he dared to compare the effect women get from these novels as similar to the effect men receive from viewing pornography—after all, isn't it true that men are excited by visual stimulation while women are excited by emotional stimulation? John was on to something. There is a lot of romance going on…in all the wrong places.

According to the Romance Writers of America, 64.6 million Americans read at least one romance novel in the past year, and 50 percent of romance readers are married.[2]

After John and I talked, I began paying more attention to where I received my emotional stimulation. Yes, I still read novels (mostly Christian) with elements of romance. I love chick flicks with a good love story. But I'm also aware of the emotional high I get from these forms of media, and I make sure to focus my affections on what is real…on *who* is real. Someone who deserves all my love and affection.

It's not just the high that is dangerous, but also the low that follows when you compare your life with the characters and become painfully aware that it doesn't measure up.

True romance takes work. People get busy in marriage and in life. We work, we raise children, and we forget about the things we did when we dated. When we were young and in love and the relationship was fresh, John and I made time for each other—it didn't matter how busy we were.

True romance takes creativity. Sometimes we use excuses like time, money, or child care as reasons not to court each other, but really it's lack of creativity. When John was still enrolled in college, there was one year when we had only ten dollars to spend on our anniversary celebration. This didn't faze us in the least. John and I asked his mom to babysit, and then we went to the dollar theater and watched *The NeverEnding Story II*. We topped off the night with a cone from Baskin-Robbins and a walk in the park. I sometimes get in the habit today of believing that a date means going to our favorite restaurant, where the tip alone is more than ten dollars. But I think we'd both have just as much fun re-creating that budget-on-a-shoestring date…maybe even *more* fun.

True romance means considering the other person. What are your spouse's needs? What will make his or her face light up? Remember that your sincere efforts will be recognized.

We meet like lovers on the sly: my husband biking home from softball practice; me sitting on a certain park bench I know he'll pass. There's a shock of recognition; a smile of pleasure; a warmth in his eyes that says he likes this setup just fine.

It's all part of finding ways to make our relationship new, introducing the unknown when so much has become known. We tacitly agree to surprise each other in carefully orchestrated ways: to look the other way while one of us packs a birthday picnic, disappears down a bookstore aisle and reappears with a package under one arm, or tosses a gift catalog our way and casually asks which items we like.

As your marriage ripens you'll adopt such little tricks. The fact that both of you know it is half the fun: It shows that each of you is committed to keeping romance alive. Is there any greater aphrodisiac?[3]

MY TAKE ON IT

True romance is messy! For example, candles all over the room catch real houses on fire, and chocolate paint is purely a fun idea. True romance also takes time to develop beyond the flash feelings of sexuality. Knowing what makes your spouse's eyes dance requires an investment in their heart that happens only in the safety of a committed-for-life relationship and by being a student of your spouse.

—Amy, born in 1970

Georgia, married twelve years

In the movies, they make it seem like the couple lives happily ever after with no effort. In real life, the couple has to work very, very hard to keep that flame going, or it will die out. You don't see what happens the next day after the movie has ended.

—Leticia, born in 1970

Arkansas, married thirteen years

Unmet expectations kill romance. That and kids yelling at you from outside a locked bedroom door.

—Angela, born in 1977

Idaho, married seven years

God gives us examples of love in the Bible. First Corinthians 13:4: "Love is patient, love is kind. It does not envy, it does not boast, it is not proud." If we can remember that simple verse, it really helps us when "life" takes over and we start getting disgruntled with each other. I think that today's society uses the word *love* so loosely. It's almost like it's disposable or something. I think we see that by the divorce rate. Love is an action, and we have to work at it. I know that sometimes people are pretty hard to love, but if we listen to what God's Word says about it, then we can really understand that it is something we have to work at. It's not always easy to be patient or kind. Pride is huge among our generation. But God has provided us with the definition, and if we search way down in our hearts and pray for God's guidance, we can definitely learn to love in the way He intended.

—Kristy, born in 1971

Texas, married fifteen years

Crazy Little Thing Called Love

 ...I kinda like it.

QUEEN, THE GAME, 1980, EMI/ELEKTRA

Are you getting some good ideas about things you can do with and for your spouse? Good! Here are a few practical ways to rekindle romance:

Revisit your history

"Tell each other what you saw in one another when you first met. What was it about your true love that intrigued and attracted you? That crooked smile? That infectious laugh? Courteous behavior? Endearing diffidence? Quiet confidence?" writes Toni Poynter, author of *Now and Forever*. "I remember my husband, on our second date, asking, 'May I?' before he took my arm as we traversed an icy patch on the sidewalk. It was so unexpected—so sweetly courtly. I fell hard—and not on the ice.

"It's nice to know what we saw in each other—it connects us to a time when the energy between us was thunderous, crackling with possibility. Together, remember your common history. Sharing it with each other binds you together."[4]

Run away...together

Last January, John and I started the year by running away together to Banff, Canada, which is only four hours away. Taking a break together in January worked well for us; I'm usually tired from balancing kids, book deadlines, and holidays, and John is tired from the end-of-the-year crunch at work.

We had the best time together. We slept in, went on walks, took bubble baths, talked… you get the picture. We enjoyed ourselves so much, in fact, that we're planning another January weekend getaway this year. I'm hoping it turns into an annual tradition!

Remember and **R**eflect

"Tomorrow morning, get your eyes off the toast…long enough to LOOK at your spouse…. Look at his or her hands," writes Dr. Ed Wheat, author of *Love Life for Every Married Couple*. "Do you remember when just to look at those hands made your heart lift? Well, LOOK…and remember. Then loose your tongue and tell him or her how you feel…. Ask the Lord to give you a sentimental, romantic, physical, in-love kind of love for your spouse. God will do this. His love in us can change the actual physical quality of our love for our spouses."[5]

I love how Ed Wheat urges readers to go beyond remembering to *reflecting*. Don't keep your warm thoughts to yourself; speak them to your spouse. Also, express them as thankfulness to God. The apostle Paul wrote, "Every time you cross my mind, I break out in exclamations of thanks to God" (Philippians 1:3, MSG). Can you imagine how much love you would feel toward your spouse if you did that consistently? Can you imagine how loved you'd feel if your spouse did the same?

"Identify your spouse's positive characteristics and choose to thank God for these traits," writes Gary Chapman in *The Four Seasons of Marriage*.

Thank God that your spouse is made in His image and is therefore extremely valuable. Thank God that your spouse is uniquely gifted and has a unique role to play in the kingdom of God. Thank God that marriage was His idea and ask Him to give you the ability to be His messenger by communicating positive statements to your spouse. Then begin to express appreciation for the positive traits you observe in your spouse.

You can choose a winning attitude even when your spouse shows no interest in improving your marriage.[6]

Relate

To me, romance means wooing. Nothing solicits my affections more than when John puts my needs above his. And you know what? It makes me want to return the gesture, simply out of consideration.

Make my joy complete by being like-minded, having the same love, being one in spirit and purpose. Do nothing out of selfish ambition or vain conceit, but in humility consider others better than yourselves. Each of you should look not only to your own interests, but also to the interests of others. Your attitude should be the same as that of Christ Jesus. (Philippians 2:2–5)

Jesus gave everything to show us His love. When I think about this, I realize that giving John a back rub doesn't sound too difficult or sacrificial after all.

My Take on It

Nothing says "I love you" more than washing the dishes.

—Stacey, born in 1975

California, married four years

Some people think love is a thing, something you can possess. Others think love is a feeling. But love is an action. It is a verb. Love is something you do. If you really want to love your husband, pick up his socks.

—Jennifer, born in 1969

Wisconsin, married thirteen years

Take My Breath Away

My love, take my breath away.

BERLIN, *TOP GUN* SOUNDTRACK, 1986, COLUMBIA RECORDS

It has been said, "The goal of marriage is two-fold: to reveal the glory of God and to enhance the glory of one's spouse."[7] Yet why is this second half so hard? Why do we find it so difficult to be our spouse's biggest fan, cheering him or her on and offering the gift of affirming words?

Of course, words are only the beginning. What our moms told us is also true: "Actions speak louder than words." Our love can open wonderful possibilities, and cheering on our spouse can bring amazing growth to many levels of our relationship.

> One miracle of marriage is that we discover in ourselves and in our partner a true desire to help the other person become his or her best self. I think it is the part of us that is most noble, even the most godly, because it is about creat- ing—not in our own image, but in the image of God we see in one another. It is love that draws this from us: an intimation of the divine pushing us to realize our potential and to help our partner to do the same.[8]

Right now, as I think about helping John become his best self, the weeks are counting down toward the Super Bowl. It makes me think about what a great time it will be to snuggle next to John's side and observe. Not the game, but the devoted fans who flock to the stadium.

Here are a few traits of a devoted fan:

1. A devoted fan sits as close as possible, mesmerized. Am I that focused on my spouse?
2. A devoted fan shouts words of encouragement. The player has fumbled and is feeling discouraged; the fan reacts by cheering, "You'll do better next time!" What praise do I give when John feels he's messed up?

3. A devoted fan will boo the opponent. Life's offender, Satan, is trying constantly to ruin my spouse's game plan. I can put this enemy in his place through prayer.

4. A devoted fan will issue affirmation. "In marriage, each partner is to be an encourager rather than a critic, a forgiver rather than a collector of hurts, an enabler rather than a reformer," say authors H. Norman Wright and Gary J. Oliver in *How to Change Your Spouse (Without Ruining Your Marriage)*.[9] "Keep going! You can do it!" a fan calls. How often do I offer intense words of dedication?

5. A devoted fan celebrates. This reminds me to applaud John in every victory, even the small ones, as if it were the Super Bowl.

My Take on It

I believe in my husband. Our daughters and I are his biggest fans. No one roots for him more, believes in him more, picks him up and dusts him off more. I can read him and know what he needs to hear or not hear. When I'm not sure, I say, "Okay, God, what do I do or say now?"

—Tiffany, born in 1976

Michigan, married ten years

I can see strengths and weaknesses in my husband that he can't. I point out his wins when he feels like a failure, and I suggest even more ways he can improve when he thinks he's got it made. We are like a brick and a balloon. When one of us starts to float away, the other can keep us grounded, and if one of us sinks too low, the other can lift us up.

—Angela, born in 1977

Idaho, married seven years

AND ONE MORE THING...

The deepest principle in human nature is the craving for appreciation.

—William James

The supreme happiness in life is the conviction that we are loved——for ourselves, or rather, in spite of ourselves.

—Victor Hugo

MY TAKE ON IT

When we were literally so broke we couldn't afford groceries, my husband snuck and bought me a computer. (I had finally accepted God's call to be a writer.) He didn't tell me what he'd gotten me, but he gave me a card; inside was a typed piece of paper that said this:

1.73 GHz processor	120 watt speakers
512 MB ram	56K fax modem with voice
80 MB hard drive	1.44 MB floppy drive
32 MB video card	Mouse
16x DVD ROM	Internet keyboard
40x12x48 CD RW	USB Ports
Sound card	

Underneath was a second sheet of paper that read:

Happy Birthday!!!! This is for the writer that I know you will become. This is a way I felt like I could help you reach one of your dreams...

Love, Chris

A year later, I was published in two national magazines. Plus, I was writing every month for a local free paper. I was also working on my fiction. He never let me give up. He never let me throw away my dreams and try for a "real job."

—**Tiffany, born in 1976**

Michigan, married ten years

My husband has stood by me steadfastly through each challenge I've thrown our way. Law school while working? No problem. Kids? No problem. Writing? Absolutely. You name it, he's supported me and believed in me at the times when I was convinced it was all over and I was destined to fail.

—Cara, born in 1974

Indiana, married eleven years

Clash Points Around Feedback:

Traditionalists: "No news is good news."

Baby Boomers: "Feedback once a year, with lots of documentation!"

Generation Xers: "Sorry to interrupt, but how am I doing?"

Millennials: "Feedback whenever I want it at the push of a button."[10]

12

If You Don't Know Me by Now

Different by Design

You should understand me like I understand you

SIMPLY RED, PICTURE BOOK, 1985, ELECKTRA

I was in second grade when my mom gave me "the birds and the bees" talk. Suffice it to say that I was horrified to discover just what lurked under boys' clothes. *Say it isn't so!* And, *That's how babies are made?!*

Even more horrifying is how many years I was married before I truly understood how emotionally different John and I are. John's need for unconditional respect is a biggie. Or how his brain works best by focusing on only one thing at a time. Or how sex for him carries the same emotional impact as a good heart-to-heart conversation for me.

Men and women are designed by their Creator to be unique and necessary. God created us different for a reason. In a world that heralds equality as a virtue, I've spent more time marveling over the specific roles of men and women and rejoicing in the beauty of our differences. I've also come to understand and appreciate headship and submission…yes, even in today's world.

Most of all, I'm just glad that the lyrics by Simply Red weren't accurate: "If you don't know me by now, you will never, never, never know me." It's never too late to understand and appreciate our spouse's differences. And it's never too late for them to appreciate ours.

I love this bit of wisdom from Toni Poynter in *Now and Forever:* "Your partner's quirks of character are there for the duration. They really are not calculated affronts to you. Try not to take them personally."[1]

Of course, it took me a while to understand that. I wasn't trying to annoy John when I burst out crying in an argument; I wasn't intentionally grilling him when I eagerly asked about every aspect of his day. I truly wanted a way to connect with him.

> When asked what marriage represents to them, Gen Xers use words like *family*, *stability*…and *lifelong love.* But they also want egalitarian marriages, in which they are peers, partners, best friends, part of a team. We want to have adventures, learn together, and be the kind of couples to challenge old stereotypes and succeed at a lifelong marriage of equals. We want the kind of marriages that we've always fantasized about but have never actually seen.[2]

The phrase that stands out to me most in the quote above is "part of a team." Just as with my son's varsity basketball team, some of the best teamwork happens when each player excels at his or her specific role. My son is tall and husky, which makes him perfect for the key, under the basket. Other teammates are small and fast, and they excel at taking the ball down the court on a quick break.

"In God's mind our differences are designed to be complementary, not to cause conflicts. This principle is illustrated by the Christian church, described in 1 Corinthians 12 as being similar to the human body—composed of ears, eyes, legs, feet, hands, arms, and so forth. Each member of the church is seen as an important part of the body. When everyone works in unity, each part enhances the others and together they serve the purposes of God," writes Gary Chapman.

"Similarly, in the institution of marriage, God intends for husbands and wives to bring their unique characteristics together to form one team that will work together under God's direction to accomplish his eternal purposes. God designed our differences to be assets, not liabilities. When we learn to maximize our differences for the benefit of the marriage, we align our lives with God's purposes."[3]

Just what are these assets? How can the roles of men and women work together for good? This is a good place to talk about biblical hierarchy—or what some call headship and submission, although I prefer the first term. I'll be nice and let boys go first.

Boys Don't Cry

...took you for granted.

THE CURE, BOYS DON'T CRY, 1980, FICTION RECORDS

It may be true that boys don't cry (often), but they do ache when we take their call and their responsibility for granted. Or worse yet, when wives buck the system and then *still* point to their husbands when things go wrong. In his book and video series *Love and Respect*, Emerson Eggerichs writes:

> The passage that spells out biblical hierarchy is Ephesians 5:22–24: "Wives, be subject to your own husbands, as to the Lord. For the husband is the head of the wife, as Christ also is the head of the church, He Himself being the Savior of the body. But as the church is subject to Christ, so also the wives ought to be to their husbands in everything" (NASB).
>
> In some translations, the words "be subject to" are translated "submit." The Greek word here is *hupotasso*, a compound word that means to rank under or place under. God is not giving husbands some carte blanche label of "superior"; He is giving husbands a tremendous responsibility, as Paul clearly points out in the next few verses: "Husbands, love your wives, just as Christ also loved the church and gave Himself up for her, so that He might sanctify her, having

cleansed her by the washing of water with the word, that He might present to Himself the church in all her glory, having no spot or wrinkle or any such thing; but that she would be holy and blameless" (verses 25–27).

Here the responsibilities of being "head" are clearly spelled out. The husband is given the awesome responsibility to love his wife just as Christ loved the church and gave Himself up for her. That is why the good-willed husband who understands this passage sees it as his duty to protect his wife. At the same time, the wife is called upon to place herself under that protection. This is the biblical definition of hierarchy. It is not male superiority for the sake of putting down the female. It is the male's responsibility to place himself over the female and protect her.[4]

Eggerichs also talks about how natural and easy it is for wives to understand this concept of responsibility and protection. For example, if I hear a noise in the house in the middle of the night, I wake John up and ask him to check it out. If the car gets a flat tire, I call him and I count on him to come rescue me. If we run short on money to pay the bills, I look to John for the answer.

But I have a harder time dealing with the other aspect that is naturally joined with responsibility: authority.

"No smoothly running organization can have two heads," writes Eggerichs.

To set up a marriage with two equals at the head is to set it up for failure. That is one of the big reasons that people are divorcing right and left today. In essence, these marriages do not have anyone who is in charge. God knew someone had to be in charge, and that is why Scripture clearly teaches that, in order for things to work, the wife is called upon to defer to her husband.

Wives often tell me that if they submit to their husbands, it means burying their brains and becoming a doormat. If you want to work with your husband to reach mutually satisfying decisions most of the time, follow this principle: Go on record with your husband that you see him as having 51 percent of the responsibility and, therefore, 51 percent of the authority.[5]

Will looking to your husband's opinions be hard? Yes. Will giving him final say in decisions be tough? You bet. Should we expect marriage to always be easy? Uh, no. Can we expect to always enjoy our differences and never experience the pain of not having our way? No again, but I know I've been blessed when I follow God's design. Besides, whoever said marriage would be easy?

In the anthology *Generations: A Century of Women Speak About Their Lives,* a ninety-two-year-old woman says, "Today a lot of marriages break up because people are not willing to recognize certain differences in their characters and make compromises. I don't think there's enough willingness to put up with the pain and differences in a marriage. You can't have a relationship with a person for a lifetime and be a complete human being yourself without painful things happening. They have to be faced and handled. Today's human beings, I think they are too frivolous about this. Marriages fall apart too easily. It is very sad. It's preposterous."[6]

When you think about it, wives expecting their husbands to be responsible but not giving them the authority to make decisions *does* sound preposterous, doesn't it? Maybe God knew what He was talking about when it comes to biblical hierarchy after all.

MY TAKE ON IT

I can submit to my husband's leadership when I understand that he has the harder role. He is to love me as Christ loves the church, even when I am unlovable. I am to submit to his leadership because I understand that God will hold him accountable for the decisions he makes. In a way, being under his leadership is protection for me. At the same time submission does not mean that I chuck my intelligence and opinion out the door. As a submissive wife, I am to pray about decisions, give my husband my opinion about what I think we should do, wrestle it out with him if we are in disagreement, and then ultimately submit to his leadership. Last summer I think I finally got it right after ten years of marriage. We had the unexpected opportunity to return to Washington, DC. We had both been offered great jobs, but for me it was almost a dream job. We wrestled about the decision together. We prayed, we talked, we prayed some more. God impressed on me that it was a decision my husband needed to make—I needed to empower him to be the leader in our home. So I told my husband that it was his decision to make and I would agree with whatever he decided. My husband made a decision, and it was very hard to submit to it. However, I knew that he had prayed long and hard about it, and he felt he had heard God. That gave me a level of peace, even when part of me cried for the decision to have gone the other way.

—Cara, born in 1974

Indiana, married eleven years

Headship looks like my husband taking the lead to pray for us, to open discussion on necessary issues, and to be the chief disciplinarian. Submission looks like me taking my disagreements to God first and then to my husband if I know I have a valid concern to bring up. Submission looks like me respecting my husband in front of my children and behind closed doors. It also looks like us talking over everything that concerns our lives and praying and listening and talking some more. It looks like me doing the budget because it's my strength and my husband doing the cooking because he loves to do it.

—Amy, born in 1970

Georgia, married twelve years

Earth Girls Are Easy

Promise you won't tell?

JULIE BROWN, GODDESS IN PROGRESS, 1984, SIRE RECORDS

The topic of biblical hierarchy can be thought- and conversation-provoking. But when it comes right down to it, as Julie Brown sang, "Earth girls are easy." I'm being serious here.

"God created woman to complete man, not to compete with man," writes Sharon Jaynes, author of *Becoming the Woman of His Dreams*.[7] And when I really think about it, I don't want to compete. I desire appreciation and validation when I'm doing a good job. (Gold star, please.) I want my husband to trust my intuition even when I don't have facts and stats to back up what I'm feeling. I want my strengths to be appreciated too. All of them, even the ones I don't recognize as strengths.

"When the man is weak, his wife is strong; when she stumbles, he is there to pick her up. Life is easier when two hearts and minds are committed to working together to face the challenges of the day," says Gary Chapman, author of *The Four Season of Marriage*.

Yes, women are complicated, but in the end we want only one thing—to be *treasured, cherished, adored, pursued*. I think our husbands would understand us better if they knew this:

> Think of the deals you've struck in your life. Your first car. Your first real job. Your first house. You saw what you wanted, did what you had to do to get it—and you came home with a done deal.
>
> No deal compares to winning a wife, though. You pursued her with all the creativity and resources you could muster, and the deal was done. Your wedding day was the day you proved your love to the world, and to her.... Marriage feels like the most obviously *closed deal* in your whole life.
>
> Right?
>
> Well, not exactly.... It just feels closed for you.
>
> No, your wife isn't still out looking for other suitors. But in an unusual and powerful way that married men don't really understand, your wife doesn't feel permanently loved once the marriage papers are signed. Yes, she *knows* you love her, but there are periodic times when her *feelings* need to be convinced and reassured.[8]

Men may think we're crazy, but we can never be convinced and reassured enough. Just as we regularly experience hunger for food (and coffee and chocolate), we are hungry for reassurance.

Do you still love me? we wonder every day. (At least I do.)

Do you think I'm wonderful? Even though we don't ask, we want to.

When I'm mad, I wonder these things. When I'm happy too. When I make dinner. When I sweep the floor. When I feel fat. When I fix my hair and look nice. When I get dressed up. When I get naked. When I accidentally get a ding in the car. When I forget to make a bank deposit as he asked. When I come home with a bagful of clearance items.

I don't mean to be insecure, but I am. I know my husband loves me, but I want to hear it, see it, *and feel it.*

Perhaps you wonder why I've chosen to discuss our need to be cherished in this chapter rather than in the chapter on romance. It's because to me, it's not romance. It's a daily need, just like air. And for some reason, God made women this way. We are different by design. And when we are loved like this, we cling to our lover, whether it is God or our spouse.

"It's common for men to think that pursuing goes with dating, not marriage. But women don't see things that way. There is never that magic moment of closure when they feel permanently, fully, deeply loved. *They think that's what the rest of married life is for!* That's why they need and deserve to be pursued every day," Shaunti and Jeff Feldhahn write in *For Men Only.* "In fact, several women compared the need to feel pursued by their husbands with the need that a man has to feel sexually desired by his wife! If it's that important, what is a smart married man to do?

"Big-screen answer: Give chase.

"Pixel answer: Ask yourself, *What did I do when I was dating that made me so pickin' irresistible?*"[9]

Lastly, I think appreciating our differences all comes down to one thing: trust. We have to trust that God designed men and women differently for a reason. We have to trust that our spouse does love us and has our best interests in mind.

God made men to rise to the challenge of responsibility and crave authority. He gave women a desire to be pursued. When you embrace these differences and meet the needs of the other, watch out. You will have a marriage that *shines.* One that displays God's design, brings Him glory, and is filled with a whole lot of joy too.

MY TAKE ON IT

Marriage is like a dance: Someone has to lead. By design, it is the man. If the man leads and the woman follows, they twirl around the floor and everyone watches. They rise and fall with the music. They never bump into anyone or step on each other's feet. It is beautiful and they draw everyone's envy. Funny, but no one envies the couple standing in the middle of the dance floor arguing or the couple that is bumping into everyone. Of course, this following thing isn't easy in life or in dancing. As the song goes, "Dancing backward in high heels" isn't easy. But when done right, it is a beautiful thing. Even with all the books I've read and all my effort, it is still hard to honor my husband's God-given position in our family. In the end, it is only by God's grace that I can be the wife He wants me to be.

—Jennifer, born in 1969

Wisconsin, married thirteen years

I love that my husband respects my intuition and that I'm a mom who loves my kids as only a mom can. I love that my husband loves and teaches our girls and leads our home as only a man after God's heart can. That we both love and respect each other and have the freedom to use the strengths God has given each of us makes our marriage a safe place that doesn't have to look like the Joneses.

—Amy, born in 1970

Georgia, twelve years

And One More Thing...

He Said:

> You have stolen my heart, my sister, my bride;
>> you have stolen my heart
> with one glance of your eyes,
>> with one jewel of your necklace.
> How delightful is your love, my sister, my bride!
>> How much more pleasing is your love than wine,
>> and the fragrance of your perfume than any spice!
> Your lips drop sweetness as the honeycomb, my bride;
>> milk and honey are under your tongue.
>> The fragrance of your garments is like that of Lebanon.
> You are a garden locked up, my sister, my bride;
>> you are a spring enclosed, a sealed fountain. (Song of Songs 4:9–12)

She Said:

> His arms are rods of gold
>> set with chrysolite.
> His body is like polished ivory
>> decorated with sapphires.
> His legs are pillars of marble
>> set on bases of pure gold.
> His appearance is like Lebanon,
>> choice as its cedars.
> His mouth is sweetness itself;
>> he is altogether lovely.
> This is my lover, this my friend,
>> O daughters of Jerusalem. (Song of Songs 5:14–16)

13

LOVE IS A BATTLEFIELD

Conflict Resolution for Couples

You're a real tough cookie with a long history.

PAT BENATAR, BEST SHOTS, 1989, CAPITAL

Unlike the television sitcoms Gen Xers grew up watching, conflict in our relationships doesn't wrap up in thirty minutes with everyone smiling at the end.

When I think about the conflicts John and I have experienced in the past, I recognize that they come down to one thing: selfish thinking by one or both of us.

"Selfishness probably kills more marriages than anything else, including adultery (which is selfishness crawling along slimy depths). Selfishness speaks of *my* identity, *my* rights, *my* fulfillment, *my* happiness."[1]

It is an easy vice to succumb to. But we all know that no matter how hard it is, in marriage we need to be *other*-centered, not self-centered.

"Most marriages run into trouble when husbands and wives make two mis-takes: they *stop* doing things that strengthen the relationship, and they *start* doing things that hurt it," writes Dr. Greg Smalley, author of *The Marriage You've Always Dreamed Of*. "Repeated disappointments, arguments, and frustrations lead to con-flict, negativity, and dullness."[2]

If we took the time to stop and think about it, we could identify specific actions, words, or attitudes that signify either a thumbs-up or a thumbs-down toward our spouse.

In other words, when it comes to our words and actions, there is no sideways thumb! We are always either strengthening or hurting our relationship. The tricky part is the fact that "strengthening" sometimes appears as conflict—when it arises, we see it as harmful when in truth it is often just the opposite.

Incredibly, conflict is part of God's plan for marriage. Look at what the Bible says:

> Moreover [let us also be full of joy now!] let us exult *and* triumph in our troubles *and* rejoice in our sufferings, knowing that pressure *and* affliction *and* hardship produce patient *and* unswerving endurance.
>
> And endurance (fortitude) develops maturity of character (approved faith and tried integrity). And character [of this sort] produces [the habit of] joyful and confident hope of eternal salvation. (Romans 5:3–4, AMP)

According to these verses, conflict is really for the better, right? Looking back at the conflict in my marriage, I have to admit this is true. Through conflict, I have learned to endure and be patient. My character has developed, and I have grown closer to John.

Conflict has also increased my hope in God as I learned to seek Him and get the focus off myself. I have learned that I need *more* of God to be the type of wife John deserves.

Such hope in God never disappoints, deludes, or shames us. The more we lack, the more room God has to work. The first challenge comes in believing that matu-rity and character are worth the struggle. The second is seeing as God sees.

It reminds me of those children's books with the cutout windows: When you open the book and look through the window, you see only a small portion of the larger picture. Then, when you turn the page, the entire picture is revealed and you see how the smaller part fits into the whole.

In the midst of conflict, I have to remind myself that my perspective is like peering through a very small window (admittedly, this can be difficult when John and I are having a heated debate).

But God sees the complete picture. He sees how, through conflict, we learn resolution. We learn not to be demanding or selfish. We learn to consider others better than ourselves. We know how to react better next time—*if* we choose to work through it…*if* we choose not to withdraw.

Habitual withdrawal as a way to cope with conflict is a high predictor of divorce. Why? If spouses withdraw from a conflict, they don't ever solve it. They might try to work out the problem separately or hit the Reset button and try to return the relationship to the status quo, but they never solve anything. And in time that often leads to divorce.

Withdrawal may not look like one of the most damaging relationship germs, but it is. …When someone withdraws from conflict, he or she only delays the inevitable. It doesn't help to leave the battlefield and go out for a long jog; in fact, this usually makes things worse. When we avoid conflict, we merely brush the hurt under the rug of our soul. Eventually the mound of hurt gets so big that it starts spilling out the sides—and what seeps out often looks a lot like anger, bitterness, depression, drug and alcohol abuse, eating disorders, or worse.[3]

I've seen many couples give in to resignation. In fact, I grew up in a home like that for many years. I never saw my parents have screaming fights. Yet I never really saw them laughing, talking, or having fun together either. After a while, it seemed as if they didn't care.

It has taken time for me to realize that lack of conflict in a marriage should not be the goal. No one wants an emotionless marriage, but rather one in which the conflict is as carefully tended to as the romance, the care, and the consideration.

MY TAKE ON IT

I am an avoider—I avoid conflict at all costs! When I'm upset, I need time and space to mull over my thoughts and calm down, while he wants to address the issue immediately. My husband is a no-holds-barred confronter, and I am more reserved.

—Stacey, born in 1975

California, married four years

My mom was a yeller. That was how she handled conflict—yelling at the top of her lungs and usually slamming the door really hard (repeating it if it wasn't hard enough the first time). I didn't really learn healthy ways to handle conflict. Because of that, I tend to fear conflict and end up crying at the slightest little things.

—Michelle, born in 1971

Ohio, married thirteen years

The Heat of the Night

I was caught in the crossfire of a silent scream

BRYAN ADAMS, *INTO THE FIRE*, 1986, A&M

Are you feeling the heat? The first thing to do is figure out the origin of conflict in your marriage.

Sometimes it is clearly internal: We have an inner sense that something is wrong. This may stem from unrealistic expectations, such as fantasizing about a perfect marriage or family, like in a Norman Rockwell painting. But life, as we all know, is not perfect.

Other times, conflict arises from external circumstances. Little things, such as overcommitments or financial struggles, cause us to get upset over situations that most likely wouldn't bother us on days when we're at peace and well rested.

"The most common mistake couples make is allowing negative emotions to dictate their behavior," says Gary Chapman, author of *The Four Seasons of Marriage*. "By failing to recognize the power of a positive attitude, they fail to achieve their marriage's highest potential."[4]

One day John and his co-workers had to work late. I was a little upset, but not half as creative as John's co-worker's wife, who sent this note in with her husband: "Please excuse my husband by 8:00 p.m. Total compliance is necessary due to his wife-threatening condition."

It made me think about how often I turn little disagreements, misunderstandings, or unfulfilled expectations into a "wife-threatening condition." Too many times to count!

Of course, there are times when conflict involves more than a bad attitude. Tough stuff happens within marriage, including addictions and infidelity. And while I would never encourage a spouse to stay in a relationship where there is abuse, in most cases we turn our backs on our vows for far less.

"There are a lot of marriages today that break up just at the point where they could mature and deepen," writes author Madeleine L'Engle. "We are taught to quit when it hurts. But often, it is the times of pain that produce the most growth in a relationship."[5]

Something I try to remember is that John and I are on the same team. Winning an argument, or getting my way, should not be the goal. If we win, we win together; if we lose, we both suffer.

When it comes to conflict, here are two important things to remember:

1. **Closeness fosters conflict.** When you open your heart to your spouse, you can no longer hide your struggles. "People crave closeness with one another, but are repelled by the sin that such closeness inevitably uncovers in themselves: the selfish motives that are unmasked, the pettiness that

spills out, the monstrous new image of self that emerges as it struggles so pitifully to have its own way," says Mike Mason, author of *The Mystery of Marriage*.[6] With closeness comes love...love that overlooks offenses. Love that helps us to grow in our weaknesses.

2. Through conflict, we can grow closer to our spouse and to God. When I have conflict in my marriage, God's Spirit prods me to repent. With repentance comes humility, and though it hurts, I admit my mistakes and my brokenness to John. When I approach him after messing up (which I've had to do more times than I want to admit), I give him a glimpse inside me. Sure, it is a glimpse of my sinful human nature, but it is an honest glimpse all the same. And as John looks into my brokenness, an amazing thing happens. Conflict becomes the doorway to intimacy.

Confession before my husband is a big step for me. As I mentioned earlier, my natural tendency is to hide or withdraw. Thankfully, the more time I spend with John, the more I learn to trust his heart. I know that he wants our marriage to work as much as I do. He may not be happy with me, but I've learned to trust that John's not going to give up on me—on us. And through this learning process, John has also come to trust my heart.

As spouses learn from each other, they discover trigger points. They learn that conflict sometimes stems from miscommunication or seeing things differently as men and women. For example, I tend to get defensive when John comments on anything within my realm—an unpaid bill, a messy house, or an overpacked schedule. Because I control these things and put a lot of time and energy into them, a negative comment from John sometimes feels like a personal attack on *me*—which isn't the case at all.

On the other hand, John gets hurt when I disagree with him in front of other people. I may be right, but contradicting him before others is never a good idea. As a man who desires respect (as all men do), John views these incidents—no matter how minor they may be—as my being disrespectful.

As we talk through our issues and share our feelings, John and I have come to understand each other better. We realize that if one of us feels unloved or disrespected in a situation, we need to stop, replay the scene, try to figure out what happened, and pinpoint where exactly our emotions came from.

By opening up and talking to each other, one of the things we've come to understand is that the past sometimes still affects the present.

> Sometimes you will run headlong into your partner's pain. You may not realize it until you're blasted with reaction—perhaps a flash of deflective anger, or stony silence. When your partner's response seems inappropriate or out of proportion to the situation, it's a cue that you may be confronting very old fears or beliefs, often learned in childhood—always learned the hard way. Use these as clues. They are valuable opportunities, not as insights for gaining leverage, but to see more deeply into your partner. Volatility is a sign that you've touched a nerve in your partner, viewing a place that few ever see. Rather than press your advantage, tread respectfully and ask rather than demand. Let change unfold as your partner can tolerate it.[7]

Over time, John has come to understand how I handle conflict. He recognizes my triggers. He sees how I react and why. The same is true with me for him.

Through growth and learning, facing up to our mistakes becomes easier. Through struggles, we butt heads and then join arms again, in the process learning new things about each other and the grace given to us by God.

> Conflict is not something to be avoided but something to be navigated. If we want to get to the deeper levels of a relationship, we have to go *through* conflict. By entering the door of conflict, we learn more about each other and our relationship.[8]

Sometimes conflict builds up over years, but other times it hits us when we least expect it. One of the most challenging things about married life is learning to forsake independence for interdependence. It's not me against John; rather it's *us against the world.* When married partners solve problems together, they grow closer instead of letting challenges get the best of them.

My Take on It

My husband and I have set ground rules for conflict: No past arguments should be brought up; stay on the task at hand; be polite and allow each other to speak without interrupting; and do not resort to pettiness such as name-calling. Above all, show each other respect.

Dee, born in 1975

Michigan, married ten years

During times of conflict in our marriage, I have learned to pray. I do not feel like praying when we are arguing, but I can't deal with our conflicts in a godly way if I don't pray about it. I have also learned that our relationship is more important than winning the fight (even if I know I am right).

Michelle, born in 1971

Ohio, married thirteen years

Guilty

Guilty, guilty, you've found me guilty.

CLASSIX NOUVEAUX, RELEASED AS A SINGLE, 1981, EMI

For me, identifying my minor failures and confessing to John is the easiest part of conflict. I feel better because I'm putting the ball in his court. The same is true for John; he feels a weight lift when he confesses to me. It's over. It's done. We can move on.

But when my offenses are "big ones" that stem from years past, confession is not always easy. I've had time to deal with the issue, but I need to remember that it's new to John. I may feel better getting the burden off my chest, but for John the issue is fresh and painful.

The same is true when John brings up a struggle that takes me by surprise: It takes me a while to sift through my thoughts and emotions and find my way to forgiveness. I like what C. S. Lewis had to say about this: "Everyone says forgiveness is a lovely idea until they have something to forgive."[9]

One thing that helps me when it comes to forgiving John (and others) is understanding what the word means. *Forgive* has the same root meaning as *give*. It doesn't mean forgetting and pretending nothing happened; instead it's turning the offense the other person committed over to God for Him to deal with.

According to the Bible, forgiving isn't even optional. Ephesians 4:32 says, "[Forgive] each other, just as in Christ God forgave you." Micah 6:8 says, "[God] has showed you, O man, what is good. And what does the LORD require of you? To act justly and to love mercy and to walk humbly with your God."

"God asks us to forgive our spouse because He understands that without forgiveness, the flame of love dies; bitterness and resentment extinguish it," write the authors of *Intimacy Ignited*.[10]

Biblical forgiveness is not about pushing a button and having the memory—or the pain—go away. Instead, it allows us to recognize that the pain doesn't have to dominate our lives. Satan wants our anger to work against us, to lock us up in long-term bitterness or denial. Satan wants us to lick our wounds and feed our negative emotions. After all, we *were* hurt. But as Dennis and Barbara Rainey write in *Staying Close*, "Forgiveness means giving up your rights to punish another."[11]

Once we turn our pain over to God, and once we give up our right to punish the other person, God does an amazing thing: He gives us new eyes of compassion. Even when the relationship has sustained damage, a sense of compassion allows us to look at our spouse and see him with hurts and wounds of his own.

"If we have really given our heart to God, then we have forfeited our right to withhold love from others," says Jen Abbas, author of *Generation Ex*. "Natural love responds to the attractive features in another person; it is a selfish impulse. Supernatural love is a conscious choice. As a feeling, love comes and goes without our control. When we view love as a choice, we are empowered to make love last."[12]

My Take on It

When I put Dan first, I can see where he is coming from. Then, even if I feel perfectly justified in my words or actions, I start to understand how he could have taken what I said, or did, to mean something else entirely. And if I know Dan is putting me first, I don't become as defensive.

—Angela, born in 1977

Idaho, married seven years

I know that I must compromise for the sake of our relationship when I see my husband feeling rejected. He will not feel comfortable and capable to stand as head of the household if he starts to feel rejected. I can also tell it is time to compromise when I realize I have been totally focused on being "right" rather than on solving the conflict.

—Michelle, born in 1971

Ohio, married thirteen years

Matter of Trust

...but for God's sake don't shut me out.

BILLY JOEL, THE BRIDGE, 1986, COLUMBIA

The last element to overcoming conflict is regaining trust. If you are the offender, this is not something to take for granted. Instead, trust is something that will return only when you prove yourself trustworthy.

Violating trust is like stepping on the plant and pushing it into the mud. Although it has the capacity to straighten up and grow healthy again, it will take time. When trust is violated a second time, it's like breaking off the plant at ground level. The root system is still there, but the trunk of the plant is now gone. It will take even longer for the roots to produce trust again. The only road to restoration is for the offending individual to become trustworthy again. If you're the one who has broken trust, you must consistently do what you say you're going to do and go where you say you are going. In short, you must live a life above reproach. When this happens, trust slowly grows to become healthy again.[13]

In order for John and me to regain each other's trust, we have—for more serious issues—asked each other for daily accountability. Regarding areas in which I experience ongoing struggles, John asks me every night before prayer, "Do you have anything you need to talk about or confess? Do you have any temptations you'd like to pray about?" In return, I ask him the same.

And it works. It works because throughout the day, whenever I'm drawn to sinful desires, I *know* John will challenge me that evening. As a result, I can choose to take the high path, sin and lie about it, or confess when I have fallen.

Given the options, the first choice is the least painful and the most rewarding—and I'm all about that. In addition, choosing to take the high road builds character and draws me closer to God. It also builds the trust that has been crushed by sin.

I can look back and see that conflict—when handled with prayer, love, and a desire to improve our relationship—has benefited my marriage 100 percent of the time. It's the unexpected oasis in the desert and one I seek whenever trouble comes.

My Take on It

Knowing I have a relationship where confession is a reality makes me far less likely to give in to any temptation, purely because I don't want to have to tell someone what I did, especially when I consider that that someone is my spouse and he will be hurt if I follow through on a temptation. Beyond being a great deterrent to sin, I believe confession enables us to truly go deep with another believer and walk with them humbly because we know we could do the very same thing.

—Amy, born in 1970

Georgia, married twelve years

Our marriage is being reborn. New birth is not always easy. It is hard to let go of the bitterness. Sometimes I just want to wallow in my own misery and remind myself of how "bad" my marriage is. But as I learn to forgive and become free of the bitterness, I am learning to love in a new way. This love is full of grace.

—Michelle, born in 1971

Ohio, married thirteen years

AND ONE MORE THING...
MORE THOUGHTS ON SIN, CONFESSION, AND FORGIVENESS:

MY TAKE ON IT

Yes, I had to cast aside a lot of preformed perceptions and expectations of marriage that came from my first (failed) marriage. I had to learn that my husband is different and is here to stay and that our love is different and strong.

—Amy, born in 1971

South Carolina, married six years

Many of us carry around the scars of the many mistakes we made in our early years. We have also been taught "acceptance of others." We have been taught not to judge. Gen Xers do value truth and honesty, both with others and with ourselves. We value reality. We want reality even if it is not as pretty. When you combine all these things, you end up with a very humble and realistic generation. How can you not forgive others when you did the same kinds of things, or at least you know you are capable of doing the same type of things? When my husband or others mess up, I try to remind myself, "That could be me."

—Jennifer, born in 1969

Wisconsin, married thirteen years

Confessing sin gives me freedom from guilt and anxiety over what I have done. Forgiveness is also very freeing in my marriage. To me, it hurts me more to carry a grudge against my husband than it hurts him. So forgiveness frees me from the anger, the self-pity, and the self-destructive behaviors that come along with holding on to resentment.

—Kristy, born in 1971

Texas, married fifteen years

It is hard for me to forgive my husband when he doesn't confess and ask forgiveness. There have been times when he has really hurt me and hasn't shown any remorse. It is hard to forgive him at those times, but I know that if I hold on to unforgiveness, I will become bitter and resentful. God wants me to forgive my husband for my own benefit. I am only hurting myself if I don't forgive.

—Michelle, born in 1971

Ohio, married thirteen years

Only people who love us can hurt us that deeply. One tough part was letting go of the fear of being hurt again and learning to trust. Also, letting go of the feeling of entitlement that I had for my anger and hurt. Letting go of that was the hardest of all, but the most healing.

—Cammie, born in 1972

Florida, married eleven years

I think relationships tend to become strained more when there are secrets. It is much better to confess our sins and work toward reconciliation than to hide them and cause unresolved tension and strain.

—MD, born in 1968

New Jersey, married eleven years

After surviving an affair and going through the long process of healing, our marriage is finally one where both of us love each other on a level that says there is nothing worth the risk of losing this connection ever again.

—Amy, born in 1970

Georgia, married twelve years

14

BE Good TO YOURSELF

Taking Care of You

Gettin' close to an overload...

JOURNEY, RAISED ON RADIO, 1986, SONY

I have always been a people pleaser. I remember from an early age wanting to fit in, get good grades, and excel.

The same was true when I had kids and got married. I didn't want to be just good; I wanted to be the best…which meant pouring myself into the people in my life. This continued when I began writing books. I wanted to be known as a star author, who was easy to get along with, always on time, and produced great work. Of course, I took on other roles: homeschooling mom, children's church leader, mentor to teen moms…

Have you figured out my problem yet?

"Caring for yourself is your God-appointed responsibility leading toward being filled mentally, physically, spiritually, and emotionally," writes Dr. Greg Smalley, author of *The Marriage You've Always Dreamed Of*.[1] If this is true, why is it so hard?

While caring for others is undeniably important, I've realized only lately how important self-care is. No, not just important—*vital*. When it comes to marriage, there are three vital aspects of self-care that few people talk about:

1 My spouse is visual, and he appreciates it when I look good.

2 When I'm exercising, eating right, and resting, I enjoy better health, peace of mind, and energy for all my tasks.

3 If I do not meet my needs in healthy ways, then I will meet them—even if unintentionally—in unhealthy ways.

Let's start by examining the last point first.

I was about three years into my marriage when I read a book called *The Total Woman*. It discussed how a woman should treat her husband so he would *adore* her. Here are some of the things I internalized from reading it:

- ✤ Make a list of priorities, and do the most important first, bringing order to your day.
- ✤ Meet your husband at the door after work looking good, smelling good, with a smile and dinner cooking.
- ✤ Never talk negatively about your husband to others. Or to him.
- ✤ Give your husband a twenty-second kiss before he heads to work, giving him reason to think about you throughout the day.
- ✤ Have sex daily (or as close to it as you can achieve).
- ✤ Compliment your husband. Cheer him on. Affirm him with your words.

Sounds great, right? John loved it. I was the best wife ever, and we had the perfect marriage—or at least it looked that way. I sent my husband off with a kiss and a smile. I made dinner and kept the house clean. I balanced my writing and volunteer responsibilities. And I enjoyed many intimate moments with my husband.

The system worked extremely well for a people pleaser like me. It also worked extremely well for someone who despised confrontation and conflict. And for someone who didn't really like sharing her feelings anyway.

Until I crashed.

In an earlier chapter, I talked about receiving an e-mail from an old boyfriend and my shock at how quickly my emotions got entangled. Looking back, I suppose I shouldn't have been shocked. Through this voice from my past, I heard things like:

❖ You are wonderful.

❖ You are still beautiful.

❖ You've told me all about your family, but what do you do for you? When do you have fun? When do you relax?

❖ Remember the fun we used to have together?

It's not that my husband wasn't telling me how wonderful and beautiful I was— he did this on a regular basis. But for some reason, those comments from my past met needs I didn't realize I had.

Sure, things bothered me about my marriage, but I stuffed them.

Sure, I wished I had time for coffee with a friend or a manicure, but there was work to be done.

Sure, I wanted to relax, but there were people who needed me—a family, church, and community to serve.

Since that experience, I've come to recognize how important it is to care for myself. To take time to breathe. To care for my body. To share my true feelings. To understand that happiness doesn't mean plastering on a smile and pushing through when I'm tired and cranky, overwhelmed and needy.

When we're doing things in our marriage that aren't healthy for us, it's tempting to blame our partner rather than own up to our part in the matter. If you're doing the laundry for the umpteenth time and furious at your spouse for not sharing the task, ask yourself, *Who expected me to do this?* It sometimes happens that we are the ones expecting these things from ourselves. In your life together, which complaints are yours to own? Identify some behaviors that don't work for you anymore. Clear them out, like old crabgrass.[2]

Looking back now, I recognize other unhealthy habits I turned to in search of small satisfactions throughout the day…namely, food—especially anything containing sugar. Or chocolate. I also see that I took on too many responsibilities and denied my own needs in order to fulfill those obligations.

These are behaviors that no longer work for me. They never worked. And while I haven't given up on caring for my family, writing, and volunteering, I take a realistic view of just how much I can do without burning myself out.

I also share my struggles, joys, fears, and hopes with John. I try to be real. And I try to take care of the real me.

My Take on It

Some days taking care of myself means allowing time to put my makeup on and do my hair so I feel "together." Other times it means giving myself permission to let the laundry go unfolded so I can relax with a movie, popcorn, and tea after a busy week. Recently a sudden rush of emotional stress took a toll on my health. God used several of my friends to show me the importance of setting everything aside in order to deal with the problem. It was so hard to get past the guilt that I was letting people down somehow by admitting that this thing was beyond me. I had to take time off from work, let things go undone, and slow down long enough to get to the core of the problem. I thank God for the people He surrounded me with who had the courage to say, "Jeanette, it's time to take care of you."

—Jeanette, born in 1967

Nevada, married eighteen years

Negative self-talk leads to *depression!* I know; I have been there before. When you give yourself negative self-talk, then you believe that whatever you do won't matter anyway, so why bother? You think, *Who actually cares if I've taken a shower today or if the clothes I'm wearing are out of the laundry bin?*

—Kristy, born in 1971

Texas, married fifteen years

I don't think working to look and feel our best has to become an obsession. There's a healthy balance between accepting who you are and working to be the best *you* that you can be.

—MD, born in 1968

New Jersey, married eleven years

Certain stores have sizes for preteens and teens, but those styles and sizes are not realistic for thirty-something mothers. Being able to find nice clothes that fit well and look good boosts my self-esteem.

—Stacey, born in 1975

California, married four-and-a-half years

Physical

Let me hear your body talk.

OLIVIA NEWTON-JOHN, PHYSICAL, 1981, MCA

I can't help it: Every time I even read the word *physical*, I see Olivia Newton-John dancing around in leotards and leg warmers. She was the symbol of beauty in the late 1970s, and every girl wanted to be like her.

As time went by, we just updated the models: Brooke Shields, Christie Brinkley, Cindy Crawford, Madonna… With comparisons like this, we could never live up to the ideals.

From the distinctly different he said/she said conversations below, you will see the effect this type of thinking has on a relationship:

She said:

I appreciate my husband's kind words. I really do. John and I work hard to instill in our children the concept of "If you don't have something nice to say, don't say anything at all." That's why it's hard to explain the times when the "something nice" John says makes me shudder instead of smile. There are times when I find his compli-ments hard to take. Very hard.

Take the other morning, for instance. I was curled up on the couch in my favor-ite black robe with my Bible. I had my glasses on and my hair was pulled back in a hasty ponytail. Not only that, but the pounds I *thought* I kissed good-bye last sum-mer had returned.

Then John entered the room. Showered, shaved, and neatly dressed, he paused in the doorway and looked at me. "You're so beautiful," he said.

"Yeah, right," I muttered.

He said:

I walked into the room and stopped short. Tricia was sitting on our couch—comfort-able, relaxed, reading her Bible. The first image of my bride that morning. She was wearing those glasses again. They give her an innocent yet studious look. Behind the glasses, her face radiated the peace of God. I couldn't help but think how grateful I was to have her as my lifelong helpmate. Overwhelmed at the blessing the Lord had given me, I paused.

Tricia looked up.

I smiled at her. "You're so beautiful," I said.

What is that look on her face—a grimace? Why does she do that? Doesn't she believe me?

I wish Tricia could see herself as I see her. Sure, I love it when she dresses up. But I also love her in her bathrobe and glasses because it is intimate to me. No one else sees her like this. (Besides…that robe does show off her curves.)

I made a vow early on never to belittle my wife. I wish she would do the same. Tricia tends to look at her faults and shortcomings and base her self-worth on those things alone. I, on the other hand, look at her virtues and her dedication in serving God and declare, "You are *so* beautiful."

Tricia used to have an obsession with pointing out all her flaws. Sure, she's not the eighteen-year-old I married, but so what? Lying in the darkness one night, I finally had to tell her to stop putting herself down. I know that if you hear something often enough, you start to believe it. I don't want that as part of my belief system.

After sharing my concerns about how she talked down about herself, I asked her to say out loud, "I'm beautiful." I was amazed at how hard it was for her.

I would rather have Tricia as my wife than any supermodel. Hollywood's concept of beauty is an airbrushed falsity. On top of that, the world's concept of "life-long" commitment can have a shorter life span than an egg salad sandwich on a hot sidewalk.

To me, beauty is seeing love reflected when Tricia looks into my eyes. Beauty is two people who gaze at each other with the same look of love on their fiftieth wedding anniversary as they did on their first. Unconditional love! That is what I want to give. That's what I want Tricia to receive. That is beautiful.

John and I wrote the above dialogue together. I can talk about all the things I'm working on to improve our marriage and I can share how wonderful John is, but when I look at myself, my first inclination is to identify my faults.

Recently, I was complaining about how much weight I needed to lose. John looked at me sternly and said, "Stop talking about my wife that way."

Ouch. I was doing that, wasn't I?

So…lately I'm really trying to do two things: (1) relax and (2) primp. Those may sound like opposites, but they're not. Let me explain:

Relax.

Marriage is different from living together, a friend of mine observed, because "everyone relaxes." Often we take that to mean negative things: Both of you drop your best behavior and start to show your bad habits. That certainly happens! But it's also true that once you relax, you become more real, more genuine in every respect. More of you is available for your partner to learn about and wonder at. The tense longings and bottomless expectations of courtship fall away. You have gotten what you wanted. Now, no longer "wishing," you're "doing." A hardy, lusty realism replaces wide-eyed wonder. You get loose, ready for anything. You're an athlete, tuned up for the main event. The familiarity and certainty that come with marriage bring strength for the journey ahead.[3]

John loves to see me relaxed because it reminds him that I am his alone…there is nothing to hide. However, he also appreciates it when I take care of myself.

This leads to my next point:

Primp.

"Seven out of ten men indicated that they would be emotionally bothered if the woman in their lives let herself go *and didn't seem to want to make the effort to do something about it*. Only 12 percent said it didn't bother them—and even fewer happily married, younger, churchgoing men weren't bothered," writes Shaunti Feldhahn, author of *For Women Only*.[4] She goes on to say:

> Most of us can get paralyzed into inaction by the thought of having to look like the impossibly thin twenty-year-olds on TV. But over and over again, I heard each man say that what mattered most to him was not that his wife shrank down to her honeymoon bikini, but that she was willing to make the effort to take care of herself for him…. Five out of six men agreed—with regular churchgoers agreeing even more strongly. It's not that results don't matter—of course they do—but they will be a by-product of our efforts to take care of ourselves.[5]

I don't need these statistics to understand why my husband's eyes light up when I take time to primp.

Marriage isn't all about caring for the other person; it also means caring for ourselves. Too many times, as the years go by, we find ourselves in a rut. Our appearance, emotions, and health concerns can be a burden or a benefit in our relationship. By taking care of ourselves, we show care for our spouse.

Sometimes the best thing we can do is also the simplest. As British physician Gregory Dean Jr. puts it, "The two best physicians of them all are Dr. Laughter and Dr. Sleep."

"Love is the result of hundreds of small decisions, each and every day," write the authors of *Love the Life You Live*.[6] This means taking care of yourself in little ways like painting your nails, doing those sit-ups, and perhaps purchasing a new shirt at Old Navy. When you take the time and make the effort to care for yourself, that care will extend to your spouse.

MY TAKE ON IT

I do feel that being visually appealing is important. (I should work more on this one.) Sometimes I feel like my spouse and I have been together so long that we don't even really "see" each other…but when I dress up and see that spark in his eye as he gives me a compliment, I know that it really does matter.

—Sherry, born in 1969

Tennessee, married six years

If you feel frumpy on the inside, it kinda naturally moves to your outside. It's always good to be constantly working on your insides and growing spiritually so your outsides stay looking presentable.

—Norman, born in 1965

Nevada, married eighteen years

Caring for ourselves goes too far when I start exercising instead of spending time with my kids. When I am more focused on how many miles I've run in a week than on the amount of time I've spent reading my Bible.

—Cara, born in 1974

Indiana, married eleven years

And One More Thing...

"Seventy-five percent of the more than 245 million Americans live in cities. We are urban, mobile, and constantly tempted to compare what we don't have with those who appear to 'have it all.' These comparisons can be one of the most lethal forms of poison for any marriage.

"How do we make comparisons? Picture the typical morning as a man gets up and starts his day. He may kiss his wife good-bye and head out the door, but more than likely she will head out the door with him—or ahead of him! They may ride to work together or each take a separate car to far different destinations.

"As he rolls down the freeway, the husband drives by two or three beautiful women who beckon seductively from billboards. One is dressed in slinky black velvet, and the others aren't dressed in much at all. Hubby walks into his office building and inhales a blend of Obsession, Passion, and Giorgio Red as he rides in an elevator full of pretty secretaries, accountants, and lawyers. He greets his own attractive secretary, who is beautifully dressed in an aerobically honed size seven, with perfect hairdo and flawless makeup. And why not? She has plenty of time for all that because she's single.

"That evening our hero arrives home and flips on the tube to relax. There it is—a rerun of his favorite show. More beautiful women falling into bed with the main characters. Then up pops a commercial, selling beer, cars, or shampoo—with even more perfectly shaped young things blessed with glistening hair, perfect white teeth, and flawless skin.

"Our modern warrior glances over at his harried wife. She is cooking dinner as two screaming kids with runny noses cling to her legs like small anchors. More than one hair is definitely out of place, the baby has spit up on her blouse, and she smells more like broccoli than cologne. And Hubby begins to think, *What's happened here? How did I end up with this?*

"Of course, it's easy to reverse the picture, particularly in this day of the working wife and female executive. She can go through the same kind of comparisons, complete with billboards full of Greek gods displaying glistening muscles, washboard stomachs, and no love handles....

"The basic problem with comparisons is that they are based on fantasy games played from a distance. The beautiful people on TV don't look quite that good up close and personal at 6:00 a.m.... A hundred years ago, however, comparison games weren't played as much because most people were too busy with another game called survival."[7]

15 IS THERE Something I SHOULD KNOW?

Communication

Growing up in the 1970s and '80s, Gen Xers developed a language all our own. For example, I can use the words *airhead, awesome, barf bag, cheesy, dweeb, preppy,* and *scumbag,* and we're like *totally on the same wavelength, right?* Amazing how it works when two people understand the same language.

In the *Love and Respect* videos, Dr. Emerson Eggerichs talks about the differences in communication between males and females (or what he calls blue and pink). For example, when a man says, "I have nothing to wear," it means he has nothing clean. But when a woman says, "I have nothing to wear," it means she has nothing *new*. How true!

In addition to the communication differences between men and women—how we hear and perceive differently—Gen Xers also grew up in an era when good communication role models were hard to find.

Personally speaking, interacting with my family was like walking on eggshells. *Who is in a good mood? Who is on the verge of blowing up? Who has time to listen? Who is home?* Leisure time abounded, but it seemed we often spent more time with media than with people:

Americans spent the majority (57%) of their leisure time at home in passive activities like reading or watching television. We talked on the phone a lot, making 1,263,000 calls daily in 1985, with over half of them from home. In 1986, 82% of American adults watched television daily, and a TV set was on an average of 7 hours in an American household. Children and men watched TV an average of nearly four hours a day, while women watched about four-and-a-half hours a day. One reason that TV viewing was on the rise was cable television service; in 1985 cable was available to 68% of all households, and 41% (36.9 million households) subscribed to a cable service.[1]

In addition to having our communication filtered through scripted characters via movies and TV, nearly half of us come from homes affected by divorce. This changed communication because there were some things we could say to Mom that we couldn't say to Dad.

Jen Abbas, author of *Generation Ex*, shares her feelings about living through that and the communication struggles that resulted from it:

I first began journaling as the result of an assignment from my ninth-grade English teacher. I was sixteen, the first divorce was a decade decided, and the seeds of the second had already been sown. Reading those journal entries today, I see that the hurt I hid was displaced and displayed through some really depressing and death-fixated poetry! I lacked the self-awareness at the time to uncover the source of my dissatisfied state, so I struggled simply to make the feelings go away. By the time I was nineteen, I had learned to numb my feelings. It took nearly a decade to bring them back.[2]

I understand what Abbas means by learning "to numb my feelings." In addition to divorce, there was a lot of scary stuff happening in our world. Things we feared but didn't give voice to. As a result, Gen Xers became proficient at sending mixed messages. We crave community and connection, but we often don't do well one-on-one. We want family members and friends close but not too close.

It's easier to ignore or stuff our feelings than it is to express or experience them. This fear of feeling causes us to build walls. In an ongoing effort to regain stability, we try to control our environment. We make those around us jump through hoops, yet we run away from any hoops presented to us. We expect others to love us unconditionally before we remove the conditions from our love. Often, we're blind to the mixed messages we send.[3]

Some of the mixed messages may be silence when we actually want to talk. Or screams when we desire a hug. Our spouse can't read our thoughts and may back away rather than attempt to deal with us as we are. Then there is the problem of talking to make a point, instead of striving for two-way communication.

"Two ways I have of talking 'at' the other person instead of 'with' him are: talking in order to seduce him into thinking I am right, and talking in order to sound right to myself," says Hugh Prather, author of *Notes to Myself.*[4]

Given all of this, isn't it amazing that men and women, husbands and wives, can succeed at any level of communication at all?

But Abbas's suggestion is a good one: We need to take time and look back at the foundations for our communication. We need to consider the traps we've fallen into as Gen Xers and as males or females. We need to figure out our feelings in order to express them in a healthy fashion. After all, if we don't know what's going on in our own mind and heart, how will we ever communicate it to our spouse?

Sometimes we act dreadfully. Our spouse puts up with it. All of us have blind spots that keep us from governing ourselves when it might do us the most good. Our partner just stands there, right in the path of the hurricane. That anyone would choose to stand there at all is a wonder. That our mate jumps into the gale with us is a testimony to the bravery love spawns. Let your partner give you a reality check when you need it. It may be the last thing you want to hear, but it could be the only thing that gets through. Sometimes we need to be set straight.[5]

Trust yourself to figure out how to communicate best. Trust your spouse. If you work on it now, just think of all the future storms that can be avoided.

My Take on It

I am strong-willed and was raised by a mom who likes to pick fights and have her way no matter what. I've had to really resist the urge to criticize my husband and give snappy comebacks.

—Tiffany, born in 1976

Michigan, married ten years

Ironically, in our marriage, he's the talker and I'm the avoider. I'll say anything to avoid a fight, so I prevent us from getting to the heart of the issue. Later, the same conflict will arise.

—Stacey, born in 1975

California, married four-and-a-half years

I struggle with communicating appropriately during a conflict. I try to avoid conflict and when one arises, I tend to cry. By crying, I am not able to communicate clearly or appropriately. Whatever I say is distorted by what my husband is seeing. He doesn't know how to take my tears. Sometimes he feels guilty for making me cry. Sometimes he sees it as manipulation.

—Michelle, born in 1971

Ohio, married thirteen years

Talking in Your Sleep

I hear the secrets that you keep.

THE ROMANTICS, IN HEAT, 1983, EPIC

When it comes to communication, the first step is to take a look at *yourself.* Don't look to your mate to see what he or she is doing wrong; rather look at whether you haven't been doing something right.

For example, when I was first married, I used phrases like "You always do this" and "You never do that." *Always* and *never,* I discovered, were words John didn't appreciate. They put him on the defensive. In the end, I didn't get my point across because those words made him unwilling to hear me.

Second, I believe it's important to look for the *right time* to talk. For example, while I'm most awake in the morning, John is not a morning person. He likes to talk at night, and sometimes I have a hard time staying awake. Ralph Waldo Emerson put it eloquently:

> There is one topic peremptorily forbidden to all well-bred, to all rational mortals—namely, their distempers. If you have not slept, or if you have slept, or if you have a headache, or sciatica, or leprosy, or thunderstroke, I beseech you, by all the angels, to hold your peace and not pollute the morning.[6]

John and I have found that walks taken right after dinner are a great time for communication. We walk on a bike trail near our home where we can be alone, without distractions. We both look ahead, which helps me. And we are both completely focused on each other's words instead of on television, or e-mail, or kids.

We also enjoy dinner conversations or going to bed early, which works for both of us. In addition to sharing the things that happened during the day, we discuss how we felt about them. This is the harder part for me. Yet we've discovered that if John talks honestly and is willing to listen, as the minutes tick by I become comfortable doing the same.

John has also learned not to be shy when trying to figure out what's going on in my mind and heart. "The more convinced you are of what's going on with your partner, the less you probably know," says Toni Poynter, author of *Now and Forever*. "Never underestimate the clarifying power of a direct question."[7]

When I give John an overview of my day, he is now quick to ask: "How do you feel about that? What were you thinking when that was happening? What are you going to do now?" These questions not only help him get a glimpse inside me; they also help me clarify *my* emotions and thoughts…which usually get pushed to the back burner in the midst of a busy day.

Of course, to ask direct questions such as these, one has to truly listen. How many times do I let my mind wander when John is talking? How often am I formulating my response, especially during conflict?

> We pay attention only long enough to develop a counter-argument; we critique [their] ideas; we mentally grade and pigeon-hole each other…. People often listen with an agenda, to sell, or petition, or seduce. Seldom is there a deep, open-hearted, unjudging reception of the other…. By contrast, if someone truly listens to me, my spirit begins to expand.[8]

Of course, what we say is only a small part of communication. Body language is also huge. I didn't realize this until I saw it in my fourteen-year-old daughter. I can read her face, the flip of her hair, the roll of her eyes, the movement of her hands, like a book.

"I speak two languages: body and English," Mae West once said. The amazing thing about getting to know your spouse is understanding his unique language—even if he is trying *not* to speak it.

So what is your body saying, even if your lips are sealed tight? It's a good thing to think about.

MY TAKE ON IT

The biggest thing we get tense about is not being listened to. It really doesn't matter if it's catching up on stuff or some big issue, but if one of us fails to listen or, horror of horrors, writes an e-mail while pretending to listen, that's a guarantee that trouble is ahead. We also struggle with keeping our mouths shut and thinking before emoting. That gets me in trouble every time, and I say things I wouldn't have if I'd have been smart enough to cool down and close my mouth.

—Amy, born in 1970

Georgia, married twelve years

It's important to set appointments to discuss things like finances or our goals for ourselves and our children. Almost like we have to set a date night, we have to make appointments to *talk* about the important things. If we go too long without actually sitting down and really discussing things without any interruptions, our frustration takes over and we usually get into an argument.

—Kristy, born in 1971

Texas, married fifteen years

Mark has said that he's seen me look like I hate him. I have to be careful not to send signals that hurt. But it's hard because I am not really conscious of it. When he is touchy-feely with me, I can sense that he needs some lovin'… He's a vibe guy. He sends out an angry vibe, an annoyed vibe, or a silly vibe for example.

—Katie, born in 1972

Montana, married seven years

I cannot stand it when my husband's body language is closed—e.g., turned away from me, distracted. I feel unimportant. On the other hand, when he's open and attentive, responsive, I feel loved and cherished.

—Amy, born in 1971

South Carolina, married five-and-a-half years

Say It Isn't So

But when you play in a quiet way, that bites it even more.

DARYL HALL & JOHN OATES, ROCK 'N SOUL, PART 1, 1983, RCA

I shouldn't have eaten those three slices of pizza.

That was a stupid answer.

Maybe I shouldn't have gotten married in the first place…I would have been better off alone.

Have you ever had thoughts like these run through your head? Maybe these are the voices you hear:

My spouse takes me for granted.

We used to be in love, but I don't think we are anymore.

He'll never change.

I wish she'd just grow up.

Every day, one-sided conversations go through our minds nonstop, even when others are talking. It translates to a running commentary on everything going on around us. This is a key factor in communication because too many times it's easy to let our words mimic our thoughts.

"In the study of one's personal language and self-talk it can be observed that what one thinks and talks about to himself tends to become the deciding influences in his life. For what the mind attends to, the mind considers," writes Sidney Madwed.[9]

I'd like to add that what one thinks about his or her spouse is also a deciding influence in marriage. If I think John is wonderful, I treat him like a king. If I have complaints about him running through my mind all day long, then…well, poor him when he gets home from work!

Of course, this struggle is not unique to us in our generation. King David wrote in Psalm 13:2, "How long must I wrestle with my thoughts and every day have sorrow in my heart?"

I've discovered that where I have a need, God has already provided an answer.

It's up to me, then, to go to His Word and figure out what that answer is. This is what I found:

> For who among men knows the thoughts of a man except the man's spirit within him? In the same way no one knows the thoughts of God except the Spirit of God. We have not received the spirit of the world but the Spirit who is from God, that we may understand what God has freely given us. This is what we speak, not in words taught us by human wisdom but in words taught by the Spirit, expressing spiritual truths in spiritual words. The man without the Spirit does not accept the things that come from the Spirit of God, for they are foolishness to him, and he cannot understand them, because they are spiritually discerned. The spiritual man makes judgments about all things, but he himself is not subject to any man's judgment:
>
> > "For who has known the mind of the Lord
> > that he may instruct him?"
>
> But we have the mind of Christ. (1 Corinthians 2:11–16)

I am awed every time I read this passage. The Spirit of Jesus knows the mind of God. That same Spirit is in us. And when we tune in, we can know the mind of God concerning every situation, including our marriage.

For me, the only thing that benefits my self-talk concerning myself and my marriage has been to invite another person into the conversation. And when we find ourselves obsessed with our inner commentary, we can ask one question: *Lord, what do You think of this?*

To heed God's Spirit, we need to understand a few things:

1. God's wisdom often doesn't match that of the world.

"For the wisdom of this world is foolishness in God's sight. As it is written: 'He catches the wise in their craftiness'; and again, 'The Lord knows that the thoughts of the wise are futile'" (1 Corinthians 3:19–20).

2. God's Spirit will always be confirmed by God's Word. When we know God's Word, we know God's thoughts.

"For the word of God is living and active. Sharper than any double-edged sword, it penetrates even to dividing soul and spirit, joints and marrow; it judges the thoughts and attitudes of the heart. Nothing in all creation is hidden from God's sight. Everything is uncovered and laid bare before the eyes of him to whom we must give account" (Hebrews 4:12–13).

3. To succeed in life and marriage, we must fix our thoughts on Jesus first.

"Therefore, holy brothers, who share in the heavenly calling, fix your thoughts on Jesus, the apostle and high priest whom we confess" (Hebrews 3:1).

"Change your thoughts and you change your world," Norman Vincent Peale once said. It is true. But it is only through Jesus Christ that we can change our thoughts for the better—to ensure that our communication will benefit our marriage.

Don't forget, Jesus can speak to you about your communication foundation. So when you journal, consider how your past beliefs affect your current communication style. Remember this question: *Lord, what do You think of my communication role models, my attempts at numbing myself, the mixed messages I still give?* After all, He was there too. Not only that; He has the answer, and He isn't afraid to communicate it.

It will take time to open your mind and heart. But the more you seek Him, the greater your longing will be for the answers in His Word.

My Take on It

My self-talk sometimes gives me an idea of how something would sound if I really said it, and I decide it isn't such a good thing to say. It also reminds me to try to be kinder and gentler. But occasionally it allows me to rationalize things that are absolutely ridiculous. That's when I have to shut it down!

—Dee, born in 1975

Michigan, married ten years

Oh, my self-talk can get really bad. I am the absolute worst critic of *me!* So when I tell myself that I have failed at being a wife or mother, I start feeling really guilty, or even angry at myself. Well, you can imagine who gets the brunt of that: my husband. Sometimes he is like, "Where did that come from? I just got home and haven't said a word!"

—Kristy, born in 1971

Texas, married fifteen years

That little voice helps me to actually say things in a much nicer manner. If I didn't talk to myself and to God in my head, things would just come flying out in unacceptable ways. It saves a lot of arguing.

—Amy, born in 1971

South Carolina, married five-and-a-half years

My thoughts give me commentary throughout the day, and they used to be the thing that kept all my anger and resentment festering. Now my thoughts tend to be a very short-lived conversation that goes something like this: "I can't *believe* he did that…oh, what, God? You tell me to be at peace with all men? And I'm supposed to respect my husband whether he did something I think deserves it or not? And I'm to love him like You love him? And I'm supposed to be getting rid of all this nasty stuff? And the enemy wants to steal and kill and destroy? The enemy wants my marriage??!!! Well! He can't have it!"

—Allison, born in 1974

Florida, married thirteen years

AND ONE MORE THING...

WISDOM ACCORDING TO CHAKA KHAN:
I feel for you...I think I love you.

WISDOM ON HOW TO *TRULY* FEEL FOR YOUR SPOUSE:

"Empathy means to enter into another person's world, to seek to walk in his or her shoes and see the world from his or her perspective. An empathetic husband seeks to understand what his wife is experiencing—her thoughts, feelings, and desires. And the same is true of an empathetic wife toward her husband. She seeks to understand his dreams, his hopes, his fears. Empathetic listening encourages other people to talk because they know they will be heard.

"Unfortunately, by nature we tend to be judgmental listeners. We evaluate what the other person says based on our own view of the situation, and we respond by pronouncing our judgment. Judgmental listening tends to stop the flow of communication—and we wonder why our spouse doesn't talk more! By failing at the art of empathetic listening, we sabotage intimacy, the very thing we so desperately want."[10]

16

DANCING in the SHEETS

Lovemaking

...lovers in the covers.

SHALAMAR, HEARTBREAK, 1984, SOLAR

If it weren't for sex, couples could remain best friends and good dating partners forever.

Yet it's that "something more" that draws us together—the desire to give ourselves to the other person, to know and be known.

Sex is glamorized on television and in magazines, the act itself even portrayed in movies. In reality, our personal sex lives rarely mimic the passion and power portrayed in these mediums. But instead of looking at this as a limitation or drawback, we need to recognize that by its God-given nature, our sex life should be about celebration, joy, and passion. Yes, even in the midst of a busy life!

I know this now. But it didn't start out that way. Everything I learned about sex before I got married, I learned from movies and soap operas in the 1980s.

From *Top Gun*, I learned that finding the right person and jumping into bed together should make you soar higher than an F-14.

From *Sixteen Candles*, I learned that only three things mattered: (1) falling in love, (2) being accepted, and (3) high school. Of course, falling in love makes the other two go smoothly.

From *Days of Our Lives*, I learned through Bo and Hope that it was perfectly acceptable to be friends *and* lovers. (Who needs to be married?)

From *Porky's*, I learned…way too much about everything. After all, the theme was finding sexual satisfaction in a notorious honky-tonk strip joint.

Just like in all the teen movies, I thought "catching the guy" was the only drama about falling in love. After that, you slept together and lived happily ever after, right?

I soon learned that was not the case.

"The world has desecrated God's beautiful gift of sex. What He made pure, the world putrefied. What He made sacred, the world made sleazy," write Linda Dillow and Lorraine Pintus, authors of *Intimate Issues*.[1]

Through painful lessons in my past, I discovered that true love and sex are two very different things. Thankfully, I'm now in a beautiful, committed marriage where I enjoy an abundance of both. Unfortunately, I can't go back and rewind—no matter how many dandelions I wish upon.

I know I'm not the only one who experienced this kind of deception. The incidences of teen sexual activity increased rapidly during our growing-up years, finally hitting an all-time high in 1991. It's pretty safe to say that we've all seen the consequences through a friend, a family member, or personal experiences.

During the '70s and '80s, sex education became near-universal in the public schools. Most programs were based on a model developed by the Sexuality Information and Education Council of the United States (SIECUS). Under this model, school-based sex education had to be comprehensive so that kids could reach sensible decisions on sexual conduct. "Limiting the adolescent's tendency to explore, question, and ultimately come to his or her own conclusions stifles autonomy and a sense of self," wrote sex educators Susan Wilson and Catherine Sanderson. Shorn of ignorance and fear, kids can learn to enjoy sex without guilt or danger. A SIECUS expert recommended "teaching teens about oral sex and mutual masturbation in order to help them delay the onset of sexual intercourse."...

The results of this approach are now obvious, seen in the number of unplanned pregnancies, aborted fetuses, and welfare dependents. One SIECUS prediction, however, did prove correct: Sex ed increased the rate of contraceptive use among teens. But as teen "autonomy" trumped teen precaution, rates of sexual precocity rose even faster. While sex educators and the media obsessed over increased access to contraception, unwed teenaged girls were conceiving at record rates.[2]

So we know *that* didn't work...but what came of the Gen Xers left in the wake of this sex ed explosion for teens?

"Your marriage bed is one of the most crowded places on the face of the earth," says Dr. Kevin Leman, author of *Sheet Music*. "It is teeming with people, some of whom you've never met, but they're all there—all affecting your sexual intimacy, looking over your shoulder, and shaping the quality of your sexual pleasure."[3]

No matter what past choices you made, what beliefs you hold, or what influence your parents' relationship has on yours, sex comes down to two people with unique needs. When you make a lifelong commitment to each other before God, things change. Sex becomes lovemaking, which God sees as a beautiful thing.

MY TAKE ON IT

I did suffer sexual abuse, and it still affects me. Also, my family's view of sex is so warped that I'm not sure how to describe that either... I just don't know how it *couldn't* affect a relationship with my spouse. It is with a lot of prayers, Bible studies, and counseling that I have been able to move beyond the ghosts of the past. Even though they haunt me, they don't dictate my sexual relationship with my husband anymore. It would be foolish to suggest that we can just forget our past happened; however, with God's help, we can move beyond the pain to freedom. I struggle with guilt, anger, and sadness that I took a precious gift and basically threw it away. When I start running those tapes that tell me I should be ashamed of myself, then it only leads to problems with sex in my marriage. I get closed off trying to "protect" myself, I become controlling (because no one is going to take advantage of me), and I withdraw (I don't have to if I don't want to). *Not good!* The physical impact of sex before marriage *can* be huge; the emotional impacts *are* huge.

—Kristy, born in 1971

Texas, married fifteen years

We can never undo the past. It can be terribly painful for me to think about my husband being sexually intimate with someone else. I become insecure in my marriage and my husband's faithfulness when I remember his past relationships.

—Michelle, born in 1971

Ohio, married thirteen years

In the beginning of our marriage, both of our past sexual experiences made sharing fully as a married couple difficult. I had been raped and while I didn't fear my husband or sex, I did fear certain acts that brought with them flashbacks. After counseling, and both of us coming to a place of deep repentance over our past sexual sins, our intimate life became much more free and open. And as we continue growing together, our sexual relationship continues to become more and more enjoyable.

—Amy, born in 1970

Georgia, married twelve years

Sex truly helps us connect on a deeper level. It is so much more than physical release (although that is part of it, and I'm not downplaying the practicality of it in any way). It's a deeper, more spiritual, more intimate connection, and without it we drift apart.

—**Pattie, born in 1969**
North Dakota, married fifteen-and-a-half years

Women want to wait to have sex until they are relaxed, feeling great, and the planets are aligned. What women miss is that sex is a way to relax, release tension, feel great, and line up the planets in your life. If you have a headache, sex might be just what you need.

—**Jennifer, born in 1969**
Wisconsin, married thirteen years

Human Touch

We all need it, and I need it too!
RICK SPRINGFIELD, LIVING IN OZ, *1983, RCA*

I like using the term *lovemaking* when I refer to sex in marriage. Any two consenting adults can have sex, but it takes committed-for-life marriage partners to "make love."

Lovemaking comforts because it releases tension. A backrub is good for tense bodies, a sexual release even better. God was ingenious in His creation. Through our lovemaking we can create life, experience one-flesh intimacy and deep knowledge, enjoy deep pleasure, and even comfort each other in times of stress or sorrow.[4]

These are just a few of the benefits of lovemaking. Of course, before you reap the rewards, you have to prepare the fields for harvest. Here are a few things that can help:

1. Understand passion.

There are times when sex becomes routine for married couples. But if you chase excitement, you chase the wind. What you have to look for is *meaning*. Passion isn't simply a hot, tingling feeling. In fact, passion can be a person...your spouse. One of the definitions of passion, according to the dictionary, is "a person toward whom one feels strong love or sexual desire."

How would our view of lovemaking change if we focused not on the feelings, emotions, or result but instead on the person—our spouse?

You do a lot of things with your spouse not because you're aroused or sexually stimulated, but because you love your spouse. When it comes to sex, the good news is that once the party starts, arousal soon follows.

According to the authors of *Intimate Issues*, "The Hebrew word for 'sexual intercourse' is the word 'to know.' Through God's gift of sex, a husband and wife receive an intimate knowing of one another that they have with no one else."[5]

So while connection and physical sensations are a bonus, true passion comes from knowing another person like no other, and that person's knowing us in the same way. Now that's something to get passionate about!

2. Be available.

The apostle Paul says in 1 Corinthians 7:2–5 that we are not to deny our mate the benefit of our body for sex. You wouldn't want your spouse to become vulnerable toward another, would you? Your relationship will be smoother in all areas if your mate is sexually satisfied.

When we marry, we actually participate in a gift exchange. The wife gives the gift of her body to her husband, and he gives the gift of his body to her. Each gives up the right to his or her own body and turns that authority over to the other. This is an awesome concept. Sadly, we quickly learn that one of the easiest ways to hurt our mate is to withhold the gift of our bodies. But God makes it clear that we do not have this right.[6]

When you give someone you love a present, you give the best gift you can find—something that will cause him or her to light up. The same should be true when spouses take time to understand each other's differences.

For your husband, sex is more than just a physical need. Lack of sex is as emotionally serious to him as, say, his sudden silence would be to you, were he simply to stop communicating with you. It is just as wounding to him, just as much a legitimate grievance—and just as dangerous to your marriage....

Making love with you assures him that you find him desirable, salves a deep sense of loneliness, and gives him the strength and well-being necessary to face the world with confidence. And, of course, sex also makes him feel loved—in fact, he can't feel completely loved without it.[7]

Likewise, it helps for men to understand what makes a woman tick. Here are a few truths from the book *For Men Only*:

Truth #1. She has a lower sex drive than you—and she'd change that fact if she could.

Truth #2. She needs more warm-up time than you.

Truth #3. Your body (no matter how much of a stud you are) does not by itself turn on her body.

Truth #4. For her, sex starts in her heart.[8]

Truth #3 might need some explaining. Here, again, is a quote from *For Men Only*, addressing husbands:

Let's start with how *you* work. Your eyes see an attractive woman, and generally your body registers attraction. Instantly. If the attractive woman isn't wearing much, your physical reaction is even stronger. It's like metal shavings getting pulled toward a magnet.

Your wife, though, is not like you. She is not sexually aroused simply by seeing you at your studly best. If you are looking particularly handsome or sexy, she *will* notice, and she *will* find you attractive. But—get this—*her body is still not lusting over your body*.[9]

This leads us to examine truth #4: A wife wants her husband to connect with her heart.

I make a conscious effort to connect with John in the morning and to think about him throughout my day. I keep his photograph by my computer, where I spend the majority of my time. I e-mail or IM him occasionally. I call at least once a day while he's at work, or he calls me. I smile when I walk past the bookshelves he made me. I recall some of the thoughtful things he's done for me lately. I think of his hugs and the last time we held hands.

Then, and only then, can I greet him at the door with a twinkle in my eye. After connecting, talking, snuggling, and feeling his love, my emotions really begin to kick in. I whisper, "Let's go to bed early."

If I'm connecting my thoughts and emotions with John during the day, I find it easy to connect my physical body with him later that night. But it does take discipline, a "training" of my emotions. When I do this, our needs are met and we both receive the pleasure God designed.

The authors of *Intimacy Ignited* describe the mutual benefits this way:

> It is as if God reaches down through the pages of Scripture and says to a wife, "Enjoy your husband, give pleasure to him, receive pleasure from him. Delight yourself in the erotic feelings of your sexual love." And to the husband, God urges, "Enjoy your wife, give pleasure to her, receive pleasure from her. Delight yourself in the erotic feelings of your sexual love."[10]

3. Plan it.

While my friend and I were chatting recently about sexual intimacy, she was complaining about the lack of time in her day.

"It's easy," I told her. "Plan time for sex just like you plan to brush your teeth at night. You wouldn't go to sleep without brushing, would you?"

You should have seen her jaw drop. Yes, sex does take more time than brushing your teeth. And no, I personally can't claim that I follow that rigorous a schedule. But the benefits to regular lovemaking are similar to those of brushing or flossing—*daily care and maintenance make all the difference.*

We make time and place priorities for a great variety of things…why not sex?

"In marriage, sex is the spice that rescues our relationships from becoming mundane pursuits of chores. Adult life is filled with responsibilities. We have mortgages to pay, yard work to maintain, laundry to clean, cars to service, and so on," write Bill and Pam Farrel, authors of *Red-Hot Monogamy.* "But none of us got married so we could load up on chores. We got married out of hope. We got married because we believed there was some kind of magic between us."[11]

Reading this quote makes me think of the popular book *Don't Sweat the Small Stuff…and It's All Small Stuff.* While I agree about the first half of the title, I think the second half misses the boat.

It's important that we don't sweat the small stuff like washing the dishes, catching that sitcom rerun, or feeding the dog. (Just kidding—go ahead and feed Fifi every day.) But it's *not* all small stuff. Being sexually intimate with your spouse will bring long-term rewards in all aspects of your life.

It is also important to be aware that the time, energy, and knowledge you put into sex will improve the results. In daily life, we take time to plan our dinner menus. We buy cookbooks and watch the Food Network to learn different cooking techniques. We purchase the necessary ingredients and set the table to create an enjoyable dining experience…so why don't we put the same effort into cooking up something special in the bedroom?

I have been speaking and writing for years about how the overcommitted pace of American families is killing us socially, relationally, and psychologically. We are simply too busy. Many families I work with could easily cut out 50 percent of their activities and still be tired. That's *not* an exaggeration. Most families who see me are often shocked at the way I can take a meat cleaver to their schedule.

When we live life at the pace of a NASCAR race, sex is one of the first things that goes. Once again, if you want to improve your sex life as a couple, you need to examine your relationship outside the bedroom. What are you doing that is keeping you from sexual intimacy?

Redbook magazine ran a poll on its Web site asking the question, "What would you do with an hour's worth of free time?" Over ten thousand men and women responded. Eighty-five percent of men and 59 percent of women answered sex—wide majorities in both cases. Just 12 percent of women chose shopping or extra sleep, followed by watching TV, exercising, reading, and eating.[12]

You can wait until daylight-saving time rolls around for that extra hour, or you can do some rearranging of your schedule right now. After all, you *do* hold the key to your calendar, remember?

And while you're at it, schedule the next interlude…and the next. Perhaps by drawing a heart on the bottom corner of your calendar? When you do this, envision preparing your mind and emotions; think how connected you'll feel to your spouse by the end of the month. Can you imagine the smiles?

4. Find fulfillment.

Take time to pause and truly appreciate the joy of sex. Relax in awe at what takes place when your body joins together with your spouse's.

God wants your sexual relationship to be an oasis for the two of you. He desires that the two of you find relief from routine and a refuge from stress by splashing around in springs of sexual refreshment. But if you are to dis-cover the refreshment that sexual love can bring, it may require that you make a change in attitude (how you view your intimate times together) as well as changes in your environment (the place where you make love).[13]

Maybe you've decided to change your attitude or environment. Or prepare the field during the day. Or pick up a book to give you tips and tricks. Or schedule love-making into your calendar, with the ultimate goal being fulfillment.

Whatever changes you choose to implement, I encourage you to *take time to enjoy sex*. Be refreshed. Before you flip off the bedside lamp, take note of the light in your spouse's eyes and the smile on his face. Savor the peace and contentment in your own soul.

Now, wasn't that worth it?

My Take on It

My husband recently stated that "sex is the one thing I share with you and no one else." That made me realize how special it is to him.

—Stacey, born in 1975

California, married four-and-a-half years

In moments of intimacy, when I am the most vulnerable, I can't imagine allowing any other person to be that close to me. It is not only my body, but my heart and soul, that I bare to my husband. It takes trust to do that. A lot of trust.

—Kristy, born in 1971

Texas, married fifteen years

When our marriage was in the process of being restored, I prayed that God would move in our sex life. He did. I continue to pray for that as often as I do for our finances, communication, family unity, etc.

—Tiffany, born in 1976

Michigan, married ten years

AND ONE MORE THING...

MORE THOUGHTS ON SEX (AND BOY, DO WE HAVE A LOT!)

My Take on It

When we enjoy intimate time together, that creates a desire to spend more time together, not just for sex, but other ways that draw us closer. That in turn creates a desire to express our love intimately, which is a great upward spiral to keep going.

—Amy, born in 1970

Georgia, married twelve years

Physical touch is my hubby's primary love language. It speaks volumes to him when I initiate intimate time with him. It shows him that I love him and want him like no other. It gives him the peace that all is right with our world.

—Allison, born in 1974

Florida, married thirteen years

My husband and I were both virgins when we married. I was twenty; he was nineteen. We'd seen stuff on TV or in the movies, so we understood the basics, but the reality was a different story altogether. Ten years later we laugh about the differences. No matter how well choreographed the TV version of sex, it is hollow and empty compared to the comfort of *knowing* that you are one with this person. You may not always feel like, "Oh, what a magical moment"…sometimes it's a quickie nooner because Grandma took the kids to McDonald's so Mommy could get some work done. But always having that same person to be able to be yourself with, and being accepted without any covering, is much more special than anything on TV.

—Tiffany, born in 1976

Michigan, married ten years

I think the biggest reason we become disappointed with our sex lives is due to lack of communication with our spouse. It can be embarrassing to let him or her know what you like or don't like. It's okay to talk about it, to experiment, and to give all of yourself to your spouse.

—Michelle, born in 1971

Ohio, married thirteen years

Sex *is* communication to my husband. If he's mad, sex will fix it. If he's stressed, sex will fix it. You name it, sex fixes it for him!

Kristy, born in 1971

Texas, married fifteen years

17

MAKE IT Real

Dreams and Goals

In a dream you are here.

THE JETS, RELEASED AS A SINGLE, *1988, RCA*

God-honoring marriage partnership is one in which we each strive to help our spouse reach his or her full potential. This includes helping him or her contemplate and fulfill heart dreams.

God has given us gifts and talents for a purpose. Gary Chapman explains this wonderfully in *The Four Seasons of Marriage*:

> King David captured the vision for us in Psalm 34:3: "Glorify the LORD with me; let us exalt his name together." From a biblical perspective, the purpose of life is not to accomplish our own objectives. The purpose of life is to know God and bring glory and honor to his name. For most people, marriage enhances the possibility of achieving this objective.[1]

It's a wonderful thing when a spouse assists us in bringing God's dreams and goals to fruition. I am a living testimony of this—without a doubt, I would not be a published author without the encouragement of my husband.

When I was first overtaken by the notion to write, I was twenty-two years old and pregnant with our third child. John was attending college and working as a pizza delivery guy in the evenings. We lived in a six-hundred-square-foot apartment and had about ten dollars a month to splurge on things above and beyond the necessities.

Instead of making fun of my dream, John encouraged it. We scraped together the money. I applied for a scholarship from the writing conference I wanted to attend, and somehow I made it there.

John was my first reader. He told me my stuff was good, even though I doubted it. He helped me brainstorm book ideas and prayed for me when I got discouraged. Now that my books are in print, he talks about them to everyone he meets—yes, even that poor businessman sitting next to him on the airplane!

In much the same way, I've been privileged to help support John's dream. After we'd been married for five years, John realized that God had placed a passion on his heart for kids. It happened by accident really. I was co-leading children's church, and John was the associate pastor of our church. One week a guest speaker was long-winded, and John came back to help me teach the kids. I'd already gone through all my materials, finished the snack, and had playtime, and the natives were getting restless. John rounded them up to tell them a Bible story. Midway through, he stopped to find a dozen pairs of enthralled eyes fixed on him.

He had discovered his passion.

For the last ten years, John has led the children's ministry at our church. He writes the drama curriculum every week, and our whole family works with others to bring the Bible alive for kids. Over the years I've made dinners for the co-writers, organized props, and purchased puppets. Believe it or not, every week I find myself donning costumes and acting out biblical stories for kids.

Now that my kids are getting older, children's church wouldn't be my first choice of areas to serve at our church. (I'm not as young and full of energy as I used to be!) Yet I continue to do it because I support John's dream. I love watching his face light up when he's on stage. I adore the excitement in his eyes when the kids eagerly share with their parents what they learned in God's Word.

The problem arises—and we see it all the time—when one person decides to follow his or her dreams without considering his or her spouse. Yes, God has placed a passion on your heart, but would He ask you to forfeit a lifelong commitment to your spouse to follow His call? That makes no sense. In those circumstances, we need to ask, *Is this truly from God?*

Better yet, consider your desires and dreams *with* your spouse.

A marriage, or a marriage partner, may be compared to a great tree growing right up through the center of one's living room. It is something that is just there, and it is huge, and everything has been built around it, and wherever one happens to be going—to the fridge, to bed, to the bathroom, or out the front door—the tree has to be taken into account. It cannot be gone through; it must respectfully be gone around. It is somehow bigger and stronger than oneself. True, it could be chopped down, but not without tearing the house apart. And certainly it is beautiful, unique, exotic: but also, let's face it, it is at times an enormous inconvenience.[2]

There were times I wished I could spend more time on my ministry passion, and no doubt John did too. But I discovered early on that when I prioritize my husband and kids, God multiplies my time and amplifies my ability to follow my dreams.

The best part about John's children's church ministry and my writing ministry is that we each took the other into consideration from the start. We worked *together* to achieve our goals. Neither of us ever stopped helping, encouraging, and cheering the other on.

Of course, it didn't begin by waking up one day and thinking, *I'm going to help my spouse achieve big dreams today.* No, it started from our first date. I can still remember the conversation we had as we drove to dinner. John shared about his time spent in the Marine Corps and what he did for work. I told him about my schooling and my hopes of someday being a teacher. While we ultimately ended up far from our original dreams, the important thing is that we listened to, cared about, and encouraged each other.

We also recognized that God had a plan for each of us. It was a viewpoint embedded deep in our souls, one that spoke volumes through our words and actions toward ourselves and each other.

Wesley L. Duewel sums up this idea well:

God has given you a background, a special set of personal experiences of His faithfulness, and a personality, and He has invested His mercy and grace in you in such a way that you can bless some people better than anyone else ever could. You are God's most perfect instrument for some tasks. You have your own role to play in the plan of God, and no one else can take your place.

You are needed by God for the task for which He is preparing you. It will take all your love, prayer, and faithfulness to fulfill God's call and will for you. If I leave part of my work undone and you fill my place, then you leave empty the place God wanted you to fill and some of the work God wanted you to do will be left undone. None of us has a right to conclude, "Well, if I don't obey God, someone else will take my place." If you fail to obey God, there will be a gap in the work of God (Ezek. 22:30). There are many unfilled gaps in the work of God around the world today.[3]

We knew that God had a purpose for me and that He had a purpose for John too. After our first few dates, we had an inkling that we should be involved in each other's plans. Our hope was that if we worked together, we could fulfill God's plan for His glory.

"Taking personal responsibility means that I give up trying to achieve my self-centered dreams for my marriage. I stop trying to force my spouse to change in ways that please me," says Dr. Greg Smalley, author of *The Marriage You've Always Dreamed Of*. "It means taking responsibility for my own emotions and actions in the real world and refusing to live in the world as I think it *should* be—a world of illegitimate and hurtful dreams. It means making sure that I don't try to force [my spouse] into my selfish dreams, but instead strive to discover the dreams God has for my marriage."[4]

God has a purpose for you and for your spouse. He has dreams for you *within* your marriage. Are you willing to take the plunge and follow His calling?

My Take on It

Any time we live with passion the dreams God has placed inside of us, we inspire those around us to reach higher and look deeper for the dream somewhere inside of them.

—Amy, born in 1970

Georgia, married twelve years

We try to line up everything we do with His will for our lives and our family. Peace comes from knowing that we have sought God for our dreams. Sometimes He says, "Wait." Other times He says, "Not the dream I have for you." And yet other times He says, "Now. Run." What a thrill to know that we're chasing after Him in our dreams and goals.

—Cara, born in 1974

Indiana, married eleven years

God equips us in many ways, but He often equips us for service by giving us a supportive and loving spouse. Two are stronger than one, and when it's service to the Lord, the two can come against the enemy and his tactics far better than anyone can alone.

—Michelle, born in 1971

Ohio, married thirteen years

There have been plenty of times in twelve years that one of us hasn't gotten fully on board with the other's dream. When that happens, we agree to pray together and separately and to seek God's best for our family. Oftentimes, God has led us away from one dream and toward another without conflict because our goal isn't to squash the other's dreams, but to be sure we're heading down the best path for all of us.

—Amy, born in 1970

Georgia, married twelve years

I Got You, Babe

Then put your warm little hand in mine,
there ain't no hill or mountain we can't climb.

THE PRETENDERS (WITH UB40), BAGGARIDDIM, 1985, VIRGIN RECORDS

While God gives us individual dreams and goals, couples should also have a mission and purpose for their marriage.

For some couples, this may mean ministering in their local church or opening their home to needy children. Still others may be called to short-term mission trips. No matter what your call, the world will benefit greatly from united, God-loving teams.

"When you reach out as a team, something good happens—an almost mystical bonding of husband and wife," write Les and Leslie Parrott. "Reaching out promotes humility, sharing, compassion, and intimacy. Doing good for others helps couples transcend themselves and become part of something larger."[5]

Over the years, John and I have had dreams that include both of us, as well as our family. For example, twelve years ago we moved to Montana, following God's call to find a quieter place to raise our kids. We decided to homeschool our children. While I do the majority of the teaching, John is the superintendent, technical support, financial officer, and cheering squad.

We also have dreams yet unfulfilled. Together we felt God calling us to adoption, which is in process. We have a dream of working with children internationally, perhaps in an orphanage. This isn't something we'll do next year, but we're already talking, dreaming, and planning. We've even taken steps to make it a reality—for example, refinancing our home from a thirty-year to a fifteen-year mortgage so that we can be financially free for wherever God takes us. We're reading books that focus on the emotional needs of abandoned children.

Small steps. But steps just the same.

Do you wonder where to start when it comes to considering God's plan for your future? Here are a few places to look:

1. LOOK BACK.

In 1988, I received some advice from my friend, mentor, and fellow writer Robin Jones Gunn. She told me that one of the best ways to see where God is working is by looking at where He's already taken us. Two questions she encouraged us to ask were, What purpose has He given me? and, What is His desire?

The next thing Robin had me do was write my personal story starting from birth to present day, hitting the high and low areas. Then she asked me to highlight certain points with different colored markers. Those points were:

1. *Key people*
2. *Key events*
3. *Key lessons*
4. *Lies*

Through this life-transforming activity, fourteen themes clearly emerged:

1. *Unwed pregnancy (both me and my mom)*
2. *Love of books and reading*
3. *Abortion*
4. *Intimacy and heartache*
5. *Longings for love*
6. *Teen in the 1980s (media influences)*
7. *Single parenting*

8. *God's liberation and transformation*
9. *Marriage*
10. *Raising a godly family*
11. *Children's leader*
12. *Crisis Pregnancy Center volunteer*
13. *Family ministry*
14. *Writing*

I highly recommend that you try this activity. After all, the messages God speaks through our past are often the life messages He builds on later.

Since 1988, three major themes continue to resurface: family, helping those in crisis, and ministry. Looking back at these "high points" reminds me that where God has been working, He'll most likely continue to work. And where John's path joins mine—our joint passion—is clearly in the areas of working with children and sharing God's love with others.

So what about you? What major events have touched your life? Where can you see God at work?

2. LOOK INSIDE.

It's good to take time to let your mind wander…prayerfully, of course.

As you begin to pray about your dreams, consider these questions: What interests are you most afraid to admit to others? What would you do if you knew you couldn't fail? What would you do if financial constraints were not an issue? What stirs your heart and makes you excited to get out of bed in the morning? What would you regret not having done if you knew your life was ending tomorrow?

When we are praying for God to show us the dreams for our lives and merely think on the small scale of what we can accomplish in our own strength, it is like going to the ocean with a teaspoon. We at least need to go with a pitcher! Then when He reveals what we are to do in His strength, we will be able to dip into His vast resources and pour His blessing onto those around us.

God has a plan and is looking for men and women who are willing to put their meager dreams aside and enter into a dream world of His making. "No eye has seen, no ear has heard, no mind has conceived what God has prepared for those who love him" (1 Corinthians 2:9).[6]

3. LOOK UP.

Now that your mind is dreaming big dreams, you may find your heart pounding too. But it's not pounding from excitement (well, maybe a little from excitement). Mostly it's pounding from fear: *God, I can never do that.*

Yes, you're right. Alone, you never can. That's why 2 Corinthians 12:9–10 is a Scripture I repeat to myself over and over:

> But he said to me, "My grace is sufficient for you, for my power is made perfect in weakness." Therefore I will boast all the more gladly about my weaknesses, so that Christ's power may rest on me. That is why, for Christ's sake, I delight in weaknesses, in insults, in hardships, in persecutions, in difficulties. For when I am weak, then I am strong.

Consider God's communication in the Bible. When He had a plan, He approached His people; they heard what He said, and they responded. And out of their obedient response, they were blessed.

One of the biggest dream busters is the sentence "I don't have time right now." Many of us choose to believe that once we advance in our careers, get the house organized, and complete all of our other projects, *then* we will have time to pursue our God-given dreams.

"Often, we convince ourselves that our obsession with our 'to do' list is only temporary—that once we get through the list, we'll be calm, relaxed, and happy. But in reality, this rarely happens. As items are checked off, new ones simply replace them," writes Richard Carlson in *Don't Sweat the Small Stuff.*[7]

The writer of Ecclesiastes also knew something about busyness—that it doesn't work. Ecclesiastes 4:6 says, "Better one handful with tranquillity than two handfuls with toil and chasing after the wind."

Chasing after the wind is fruitless. So is scurrying through our days trying to complete a to-do list that will never see an end. Only we can free ourselves from the crazed dance of busyness and allow ourselves time to contemplate God's gifts and callings, to make plans that fulfill His purposes.

"See, the Lord doesn't expect our steps to be perfect. He just expects us to be obedient, to take the first step, and to let Him do the rest," writes Sharon Jaynes.[8] She goes on to say:

> Your life is part of God's grand design. No matter how you came into the world, no matter what your past, God has known about you and has ordained an ever-unfolding plan for your life (Jeremiah 1:5). His ultimate design is for us to be conformed to the image of His Son. He uses the hammer and chisel of circumstances and shattered dreams to remove the unnecessary and superfluous parts to reveal the masterpiece within. Just as Michelangelo removed chunks and bits of marble to unveil the magnificent statue of David, so God removes anything that hinders or hides the beautiful creatures He created us to be.[9]

4. LOOK AT EACH OTHER.

"In the biblical account of creation, God's expressed desire is that the two 'will become one flesh,'" writes Gary Chapman, author of *The Four Seasons of Marriage*.

> At the heart of marriage, therefore, is the idea of *unity*.... Thus, marriage is not simply a relationship; it is an *intimate* relationship that encompasses all aspects of life: intellectual, emotional, social, spiritual and physical. In a marriage relationship, a husband and wife share life with each other in the deepest possible way. They view themselves as a unified team, not as two individuals who happen to be living in close proximity. Because the desire and drive for intimacy are at the very heart of marriage, the individuals involved become troubled about their relationship when such intimacy is not attained.[10]

Husbands and wives share the checkbook, the house, the refrigerator, their kids, and their bodies; sharing their dreams adds a layer of intimacy that is unparalleled. Once you step out together, you will discover unity as you never imagined.

MY TAKE ON IT

Since it was my idea for my husband to start a men's group, I didn't want to confess how hard it was on our family. After a couple of years, our marriage was in a place where it was going to fail completely if we didn't get one-on-one time together. It was more important that we fix our marriage, but it took a lot of pressure to get that across to him. Make sure your home is in order before you start taking extra time for others.

—**Lesley, born in 1979**

California, married eight years

When I started Teen MOPS, I never asked Dan what he thought; I just told him what I was doing. I didn't realize this until recently. I regret that. Not because I don't think I was supposed to start Teen MOPS, but because I could have had more support from my husband if I had put his needs first.

—**Angela, born in 1977**

Idaho, married seven years

Let's face it, when a woman has a passion and sets herself in motion, she can often get carried away. My husband is my safeguard; he won't let me bite off more than I can chew anymore. He prays for me *not* to have the urge to even want to!

—**Kristy, born in 1971**

Texas, married fifteen years

When my husband doesn't feel the same calling as I do, I must continue to pray. I pray for guidance, clarity, wisdom, strength, and contentment.

—**Michelle, born in 1971**

Ohio, married thirteen years

We lead a sports ministry team together and allow the young people to invade both our home and our hearts for the summer we mentor them. We both work with our church student ministry and have hosted discipleship groups in our home as well as sleepovers and ministry events.

—Amy, born in 1970

Georgia, married twelve years

AND ONE MORE THING...

[Gen Xers as parents] are pioneering a different form of marriage or committed partnership, in which couples don't necessarily both concentrate on their careers, full-time, as their workaholic Boomer parents still do. One spouse or partner will concentrate on his/her career while the other studies or takes a lower-paying job for a while.[11]

My Take on It

There have been times when we start to pursue career changes or moves that we thought were from God, but stop when one of us feels a check in our spirit. Then we take a step back and pray for direction. As we do that, the excitement fades and we see that the place we were going wasn't for us, or it wasn't the right time. Trying to go to seminary multiple times has been an example of God showing us a direction, but then making it clear that the time wasn't right. A few times one of us has pushed beyond that check in our spirit to "make it happen," and that has brought some financial losses and bruised egos… Unless the Lord is in both the goal and the timing, our pushing forward is in vain.

—Amy, born in 1970

Georgia, married twelve years

One picture the Bible gives for marriage is of two oxen yoked together. Can you imagine if two oxen were yoked together, but each was trying to do his own thing? When we marry, we become one; we are not two, but one flesh. We lay down ourselves to become something better. We put down our small loads and start to carry a larger load together. Two people working as a team can achieve so much more than one person working alone. And in the end there is someone to celebrate the achievements with. My take on this is very different from the norm. I believe that hanging on to personal goals after marriage is a mistake. If you are not growing together, you will grow apart. Couples need to set goals together and then work toward those goals together. It is best if the goals are completely new and different (something that the two of you have come up with together). But sometimes one of you must set your mind to achieving a goal that was initiated by the other.

—Jennifer, born in 1969

Wisconsin, married thirteen years

18 EVERYTHING I Own

Money Matters

I would give up everything I own.

BOY GEORGE, RELEASED AS A SINGLE, 1987, DISKY RECORDS

inancial struggle is the number-one cause for divorce among couples today.

In a culture that bombards us with advertising messages that breed discontentment, couples often struggle with wanting too much, too soon. This is especially true for Gen Xers: We expect to have the house, the cars, and the boat…*now*.

Because they grew up with so little, many Gen Xers desire to make up for it as quickly as possible:

[Gen Xers are] a group of tough individuals. They grew up in difficult financial times. They were being raised when the traditional family in America was deteriorating, but they held on, and they are ready to fight for their future.[1]

During the recession (1979–1982), unemployment rose to 10.8 percent (more than 12 million Americans out of work). Business bankruptcies rose 50 percent from 1981 to 1982. In June 1982, 584 businesses failed, which came close to the Depression record of 612 in one month in 1932. Because of inflation, overall prices rose 142 percent during the decade.[2]

I distinctly remember growing up during that era. My dad was unemployed for a while, and our kitchen had big boxes of staples and #10 cans of surplus foods. We had blankets hanging over the windows because we couldn't afford curtains. I got one new outfit for school until I got a job and bought my own clothes.

John grew up in similar circumstances. His parents lived from paycheck to paycheck and moved frequently for work.

Sadly, that doesn't mean we learned to live simply. Instead, it gave us a hunger for more.

In 1979, Christopher Lasch wrote *Culture of Narcissism*, a book reviewed by the *New York Daily News* as "a biting new study of present day society." It became a national bestseller because it struck a chord with readers who instinctively knew Lasch was right. Our narcissistic society continually feeds our ravenous appetite for self-satisfaction. Indulgent to our own needs and indifferent to the needs of others, we have become in great part a society that knows little of true self-sacrifice and self-denial.

Consider the basis for most advertising messages that bombard our senses twenty-four hours a day: "We do it all for you." "Have it your way." "Looking out for number one." "Get the best a man can get." "You deserve the best"—and on and on.

As Lasch observed, "Advertising serves not so much to advertise products as to promote consumption as a way of life.... The modern propaganda of commodities and the good life has sanctioned impulse gratification."[3]

The good thing about being married is that your spouse is the perfect person to pop your self-gratification bubble. You can't get everything your way when you live with someone else 24/7. Yes, I sometimes get grumpy when John asks, "Do you really need that?" But in the end, I realize he's right.

Marriage also teaches us to recognize our spouse's weaknesses. For example, I throw out the woodworking catalogs that come in the mail. I steer John away from the electronics section at Wal-Mart. And we never walk into Best Buy "just to browse."

I used to stress about the different cars John was drawn to. He would wax rhapsodic over one's leg room or its powerful engines, and my mind would immediately start thinking *car payment*. The next week John would be talking about a different car, and once again I'd be overwhelmed with the details. Over time, I have come to realize that his talk is just that…talk. Dreaming about a new vehicle doesn't mean he's going to run out and buy one. In fact, talking about it seems to get it out of his system.

Like anyone, our spouses have good habits and bad habits. When it comes to money, however, bad habits can be a little more noticeable—especially if they're in the form of a new motorcycle parked in the driveway or a new pair of earrings dangling from my ears. (And a stack of bills going unpaid.)

Even though we each have various areas that are a greater draw for our hard-earned bucks, there are certain male and female roles we can't overlook.

As I talked about earlier in the book, God placed in my husband's heart a desire to provide and protect. Though I love this about him, I sometimes struggle to give John authority over the checkbook. But no matter who is in charge of the cash flow, if John sees the bills mounting or the savings account dwindling, he feels as if he has failed in this area. The truth is, he's a great provider—we just have a hard time living within our means.

When it comes down to it, the amount of money John brings in shouldn't be related to the support I give him. For while his role is to provide, mine is to be his helper in tending our finances and being thankful for everything we have.

One way a wife can show respect for her husband is by being content with their financial situation. When she is dissatisfied with his provision for the family and constantly pushes for more material possessions, she is telling him he is failing to provide in the manner to which she had *hoped* to become accustomed. The woman of his dreams is more than satisfied…she is thankful for his hard work and tells him so.…

Comments such as "I'm tired of always having second best" or "When will we ever be able to afford…" or "I'd be happy if I had…" are arrows that pierce the heart and soul of a man. He longs to be a good provider for his family. He wants to be the hero for his bride. He wants to feel appreciated.[4]

It's sad to think that I make my husband feel inferior when I overspend or long for more. After all, these things are wants, not needs. A happy, appreciated husband is worth more than a dozen new outfits or that new computer I've had my eye on.

At its core, contentment is a *heart issue*. Through teamwork and focus, money can be a blessing to marriages rather than a burden. Of course, this process takes work. A lot of work.

My Take on It

Money issues cause great strife in our marriage. How to spend it, where it comes from, who wasted it, how much to tithe, how are we going to get the bills paid, there just isn't enough of it... Money. We need it, we love it, but we hate what we become because of it.

—Michelle, born in 1971

Ohio, married thirteen years

My mother and grandmothers didn't work. And if they did, it was more for socialization and not to make ends meet. Nowadays, both spouses often work full-time to pay the bills. But there are also more toys that we seem to "need": RVs, pools, vacations/trips, boats. And instead of having just one toy, we think we need them all. We now spend more money (or so it seems) on entertainment than in the past.

—Lesley, born in 1979

California, married eight years

My husband and I resist the culture of immediate gratification by not going to the mall, not watching much TV, and not flipping through magazines. But that only skims the surface and really only works if we're also spending time in the Word and getting filled through pursuing God and the things He gives us—like healthy relationships and enjoying His creation.

—Amy, born in 1970
Georgia, married twelve years

Xers seem to think that living in debt is natural. The Bible says that the borrower is slave to the lender. I am concerned that we are a generation living in slavery. My husband and I are free, but so many of our friends are not. My husband and I have recently teamed up to tackle our finances together. Our teamwork has been more of blessing than I ever could have imagined. It is great to have the freedom of a budget, and it is great to be able to discuss our finances together.

—Jennifer, born in 1969
Wisconsin, married thirteen years

Opportunities

...make or break them.

PET SHOP BOYS, PLEASE, 1986, CAPITOL

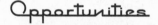

While John and I are far from perfect when it comes to money, we have taken three steps recently: commitment, sacrifice, and a plan.

Commitment involves both of us choosing to work on it. We know that when only one of us is committed to staying out of debt, our efforts become frustrated.

Next comes *sacrifice*. Nix eating out. Nix paying someone to help around the house. Nix clothes shopping...especially since our closets are already full.

Finally, *the plan*. We're working on a doable budget that includes tithing 10 percent, saving 5 percent, and managing our living expenses on 80 percent. This can be hard to do...mostly because for the majority of our married years we've lived on 105 to 110 percent of our income.

Working with a budget reminds me of something that happened when my daughter, Leslie, was four years old. She liked adding new words to her vocabulary and trying them out. One afternoon, she was trying to concentrate on a picture she had drawn while her two-year-old brother, wanting her attention, danced and sang at her side.

Frustrated with the noise, Leslie finally stood up and put her hands on her hips. "Nathan, please be quiet," she said. "You're contracting me!"

Of course, she meant to say, "You're distracting me!" But when it comes to a budget, the word she used is a better fit.

"Lord, You're contracting me!" I want to shout sometimes.

Even with the three disciplines in place, it's not easy to control my desires. However, it's a good feeling to know that sound choices today will benefit my giving, my family, and our contentment for years to come. When it comes down to it, I do want to put my family first and not let a desire for money and things overcome common sense.

Most Gen Xers agree. Books like *What Should I Do with My Life?* by Po Bronson and *Geeks and Geezers* by Warren G. Bennis and Robert J. Thomas show that Xers do not work merely for money; they want to enjoy the work they're doing. They also work to fund a family-centered lifestyle. Gen Xers expect a bigger paycheck at an earlier age than the generations that came before them, but they also want to be personally involved in worthy causes and give freely to charities they believe in.

John and I agree with all of these things…and that's why we're willing to work at it.

Of course, none of it works without communication. There are a lot of material possessions that it would be nice to own, but if couples are to find balance, they have to agree on what's most important.

It's a fact that both John and I find it easier to overcome compulsive spending when we talk often about our finances instead of just going with the flow and hoping it all works out. Living within our means entails doing without some of the niceties, such as new cars (both of ours have hundreds of thousands of miles on them). Or boats. Or even that vacation we're itching to take. It also means existing on John's income alone so that I never have to choose work over family to make ends meet.

"Money or a career should serve a marriage; a marriage should *never* serve

money or a career. In many of the failed marriages I have observed, the couple abandoned their relationship to build a fortune. In the end they had a fortune at the
expense of their marriage," writes Willard F. Harley, author of *His Needs, Her Needs*. He
goes on to say:

> The great American scramble for more goodies as you move up the ladder of
> success becomes perhaps the deadliest enemy any family faces. What should
> be primary in a marriage: your relationship as man and woman, or your stan-
> dard of living? We all know the "right" answer, but many couples still get it back-
> wards. They put their standard of living ahead of their relationship with the
> mistaken idea, "We will be happy if we can just get ahead." In many cases exactly
> the reverse happens.[5]

According to psychologist Patricia Dalton, rampant consumerism—once con-
fined to the holidays—has become a year-round American affliction. She observes
that unhappy people try to fill the emptiness of their lives through irresponsible
spending. They then consult psychologists like her to figure out what has gone
wrong in their lives.

"Those of us who lived through the '60s," she writes, "seem to have forgotten the
warning that everything you buy owns you." To pay for all their junk, people now
work so hard that they're ruining their marriages, their families, and their health.[6]

I think it's true for those who lived through the lean 1970s and '80s too. Yet God's
Word has always told us what the world is struggling to figure out. Check out these
Scriptures:

> Whoever loves money never has money enough; whoever loves wealth is never
> satisfied with his income. This too is meaningless. (Ecclesiastes 5:10)

> I know what it is to be in need, and I know what it is to have plenty. I have
> learned the secret of being content in any and every situation, whether well fed
> or hungry, whether living in plenty or in want. (Philippians 4:12)

No servant can have two bosses. He will hate one and love the other.... You cannot be faithful to God and to riches at the same time. (Luke 16:13, NLV)

Don't be controlled by love for money. Be happy with what you have. (Hebrews 13:5, NIrV)

In the end, it all comes down to holding on loosely to the things of this world. Author Larry Burkett writes in *Great Is Thy Faithfulness:*

It's not that God wants us to live in poverty; neither does He mean for us to be drawn into the allure of advertising. Our lives should not be characterized by the extravagance and foolish sensualism promoted by the mass media.

We deeply desire something, work for it, finally get it, and shortly thereafter we experience boredom or emptiness. This is why God wants to fulfill the desires of our spirits—because these other desires never can be totally gratified.[7]

Instead, God urges us to find ultimate satisfaction in Him. I know that the more I seek God, spend time with Him, and choose to be thankful throughout my day, the less draw the world has on me. When I join with John in this, somehow all our money matters fall into place.

In seeking contentment, we bring joy to each other. If we hold loosely to the things of this world, we will discover eternal riches. What could be better than that?

My Take on It

I find strength when I focus on God and the eternal riches of heaven. In this world it is very hard to do with all the advertisements about what you need to have or should have. But I have to remember that all the "stuff" is only going to burn when I die. I cannot take it with me.

—Norman, born in 1965

Nevada, married eighteen years

My husband and I have both learned to compromise. For large purchases, we always consult each other and honestly discuss the issue. We try to think of the family first, then ourselves. That doesn't mean we deny ourselves all material possessions; rather, we try to make the majority of our financial decisions about bettering the entire family.

—Sherry, born in 1969

Tennessee, married six years

Years ago our local Christian radio station ran a spot that said, "If you were arrested for being a Christian, would there be enough evidence to convict you?" It really spoke to me. Not long after that someone else added: "Could someone look in your checkbook and know you are a Christian?" I pray that God gives me a giving heart, which sometimes means give when it hurts, sometimes means give when you ain't got it, and other times means give when you have lots left over. I pray that when God looks down at my spending habits, He's always happy. Not only with my giving to charity, church, etc., but to myself too. I would never expect my kids to open a gift from me and lament that they don't deserve it and can't take it. I won't do that to God.

—Tiffany, born in 1976

Michigan, married ten years

One line of an article relating to contentment comes to mind: "What you need is what God has provided. Anything else is a want." While that's tough to swallow when there's not enough peanut butter to make it to the end of the month for my kids, the reality is that my children have never gone hungry.

—Amy, born in 1970

Georgia, married twelve years

When my relationship with God is right, the worldly temptations are just not as tempting. The blessings God provides are so much better than anything money can buy or the world can offer me. After all, only God can offer me true *peace*, *joy,* and real *love.* And He doesn't offer it to me through a new car, a new home, or the most current computer. He gives it to me through the smile on my friends' faces, the kiss from my husband, and the precious, precious words my children say to me: "I love you, Mommy!"

—Kristy, born in 1971

Texas, married fifteen years

And One More Thing...

Check Out the "Before and After" Finances for These Gen Xers:

Jennifer Lopez. Long before Jennifer Lopez sang, danced, and acted her way to superstardom, she briefly traded in her velour track suit for a suit of the pinstriped variety while working at a law office.

Legal assistant's current income: $39,130

Lopez's current income: $10 million (June 2005 to June 2006)

Dan Brown. Prior to penning his best-selling novel *The Da Vinci Code*, Brown sculpted young minds as a high school English teacher.

Teacher's current income: Median ranges from $41,400 to $45,920

Brown's current income: $88 million (June 2005 to June 2006)

Teri Hatcher. Looks like Hatcher's wardrobe included short skirts decades before she made her move to Wisteria Lane. Back in 1984, Hatcher was lifting football fans' spirits as a cheerleader for the San Francisco 49ers.

Professional cheerleader's current income: $15–$50 game

Hatcher's current income: Estimated $380,000 per episode of Desperate Housewives

19

HIGHER Love

Growing in God

Look inside your heart, I'll look inside mine.

STEVE WINWOOD, BACK IN THE HIGH LIFE, 1986, ISLAND RECORDS

Marriage can promote growth in many areas, but the most important area is growth together in their relationship with Christ. When a couple spends time in Bible reading, quiet time, spiritual retreats, and shared prayer, they grow closer to each other and closer to God.

In a perfect world, it would be easy to put spiritual matters first. However, not only is our world imperfect, but so are the people in a marriage.

Still, growth is necessary and possible. And the good news for us as Gen Xers is that we realize the importance of connecting with God.

"Our longing for ideas and beliefs larger than ourselves has led to a surge in spirituality," writes Pamela Paul.

In a 1998 poll of college freshmen, 90 percent believe in God, three fourths believe in life after death, most attend religious services, and almost half believe that religion will be more important in the future. Spiritual books regularly top the best-seller lists; Christian entertainment has gone mainstream; and Americans are seeking ways to infuse religious meaning into everyday life. Thousands of religious websites offer everything from online confessionals to service schedules to Christian match-making services.[1]

My own spiritual journey began less than six months before I started dating John, when I gave my heart to the Lord as a pregnant teen. I told God I'd focus on Him instead of guys. When a godly man named John came into my life, I promised to serve God while maintaining a dating (and later marriage) relationship.

Unfortunately, for many years it was easier to focus on the relationship with a living, breathing person next to me whom I now shared a last name with. In fact, there were times I got to the end of my day and realized that I hadn't thought of God all day.

During our first year of marriage, John and I went through the motions. We attended church and prayed before meals. In our second year of marriage, we moved to a different town and got involved in a dynamic church. It was then that our commitment to God grew. We began attending church multiple times a week. I listened to Christian music and read Christian books. We attended a Bible study for young couples, and John became a church deacon.

It was around this time that I realized something: If I wanted my relationship with God to grow, I needed to make it a priority. With a four-year-old, a one-year-old, and a baby on the way, I also recognized that in order to find time for God, I'd have to make the time.

Always an earlier riser, I started getting up at 5 a.m. to read my Bible and pray. Yes, I got tired during the day, but my spirit felt awake and alive.

"I prayed for faith, and thought that someday faith would come down and strike me like lightning," said Dwight L. Moody. "But faith did not seem to come. One day I read in the tenth chapter of Romans, 'Now faith cometh by hearing, and hearing by the Word of God.' I had closed my Bible, and prayed for faith. I now opened my Bible, and began to study, and faith has been growing ever since."

I found Moody's words to be true: Once I got in God's Word, my faith grew.

Sometimes I'd share part of my devotions with John. Sometimes he shared with me what he was studying with a small group of men. But for the most part, we considered our individual relationships with God to be solo pursuits. Of course, I longed for John to be the spiritual leader, but I really didn't know what that meant. I'd ask him at times if we could have devotions together, but we never seemed to find a "right" time.

So I went happily on my way, and he on his…or so we thought.

Even though a couple commits to following the biblical blueprints on marriage—the husband says, "I need to be a servant-leader in my family," and the wife says, "I need to support and nurture my husband and children"—that alone won't cause the relationship to "come alive" because, in the flesh, a husband or wife is not able to consistently live that way. They need more than God's Word.

It takes the Spirit of God to get a marriage on its feet! Only *in Him* can a marriage really live. That's why Ezekiel makes a second prophecy in which the Spirit breathes His life into these lifeless bodies. And so it is in your marriage. You need the Spirit to breathe life into your marriage every day, to empower you to be the husband or wife described in Scripture. It's great to study the Word of God, and you must do that if you want the Spirit to minister to you. But Bible knowledge alone will not make your marriage live. Only the Spirit can do that.[2]

Yes, I was growing in my faith. John was also growing in his. But as you know from my mention of many past struggles, this independence bled into other areas where I went solo.

Looking back now, I recognize that one of the biggest things keeping our spiritual growth from coming to fruition was my expectations. When it comes to daily personal devotions, I generally go the whole nine yards—Bible reading, reading from devotional books, Bible study workbooks I do on my own, online video series, journaling, prayer. Not all at once, but a different combination every day.

Can you imagine how John perceived it when I asked him to participate in devotions or other spiritual pursuits? I'm sure he thought he'd fail. After all, he worked full-time, volunteered, and cared for our family in numerous other ways. He didn't have the time or energy to live up to my expectations.

In his eyes, I desired a superman who would sweep down and lead our family with spiritual superstrength. I later learned that underneath his husky exterior, he felt more like the fumbling Clark Kent.

 # My Take on It

God designed marriage as a sacrifice—giving fully of yourself to your spouse and giving who you are to become one with your spouse. This sacrifice is intended to make us holy. But it also gives us joy. Today people marry seeking happiness. It places unrealistic expectations on a spouse. I'm not saying that you can't be happy in marriage, but I am saying that you won't always be happy. Rather than seek happiness from your spouse, it is more important to seek the joy of the Lord as you serve Him in your marriage.

—Michelle, born in 1971

Ohio, married thirteen years

We've tried to have prayer time and couples' time and teaching the children time, but it never lasts. I seem to be too stubborn to let the man be the head of the household. In my heart I want him to be, but it's going to take some work on both our parts.

—Lesley, born in 1979

California, married eight years

When I tried to get my husband to be the head of the household before God had gotten his heart, it caused hard feelings and actually pushed my husband away from spiritual things for a time, causing me to be even more miserable.

—Allison, born in 1974

Florida, married thirteen years

At This Moment

...what did you think I would do at this moment?

Billy Vera & the Beaters, By Request, 1987, Rhino

My Husband, My Hero

John flew into my life with broad shoulders, twinkling eyes, and yes, even a little curl on his forehead. He rescued me from single motherhood and swept me away to matrimony. But after a while, the big *S* on his chest faded, the cape began to fray around the edges, and the sunset dimmed. My hero, it seemed, flew home from work and, as fast as a speeding bullet, tackled other responsibilities.

I never told John about my expectations, but he could sense them. And instead of trying and failing, it was easier for him not to try.

What made all the difference was my finally relaxing. I stopped bugging John about daily Bible study. I let him know that if he so chose, *he* could set the rules and plan the time.

Hudson Taylor was once quoted as saying, "I used to ask God to help me. Then I asked if I might help Him. I ended up by asking Him to do His work through me."

If I could reword this to represent the way my husband changed, it would go something like this: "I used to ask God to help my husband. Then I asked God if I could *help* God change my husband (please!). I ended up asking God to do His work through my husband...in His way—my expectations and input excluded."

A man's inner vulnerability about his performance often stems from his conviction that at all times he is being watched and judged.... This secret male vulnerability involves not just a concern about what others think of them, but also the internal realization that since they *don't* always know what they are doing, they are just one mess-up away from being found out.

In fact, when doing something new or unfamiliar—a common situation— more than *three out of four* men are insecure, but don't want it to show. Only a small fraction expressed confidence in their ability to handle the task.[3]

If my situation sounds familiar—if your husband isn't "rising to the challenge" (in your opinion)—then it's time to think about the following:

1 **X-ray eyes**. Your husband does not have x-ray eyes, but you can pretend that he does. Imagine if those eyes could see deep into your heart: What would he see? How do you feel about him at this moment? What expectations do you have that he's not fulfilling? Remember, if you're thinking it and feeling it, he's mostly likely aware of it. How can you change your heart to reflect confidence in your husband's ability to be the spiritual leader of your home?

2 **Supersonic ears**. Your husband cannot hear every word you whisper, but what if he could? What do you say about him when he's not around? What things can you *start* saying to show your appreciation for his role?

3 **A body of steel**. Your husband is not invincible. Pray that he would be strengthened by God to fulfill his role, as God dictates.

4 **Ability to fly**. Sometimes you view your husband as "out of this world." Other times you clearly see the wires attached to his cape that keep him aloft. During those disillusioned times, look to the sky instead of concentrating on the wires. Place your focus on God, and thank Him for this man. Ask God to show your husband how to soar.

Many times—even without meaning to—we treat our spouse as if we are unequally yoked. Although this biblical reference refers to an unsaved spouse and a saved spouse pulling in two opposite directions, there is another kind of imbalance: when one of two Christians in a marriage surges ahead, attempting to pull his or her mate along.

The apostle Peter said one of the keys to living in an unequally yoked marriage is that the Christian should exhibit "respectful, pure behavior" in dealing with her spouse. Respect is a crucial ingredient in marriage, especially to husbands. It tells your spouse that you appreciate him, that you value him as a person, that you regard his opinions as being important, that you have faith in him, that you admire him, that you're thankful for who he is and what he does, and that you hold him in the highest esteem.

If you lose respect for your husband, you may very well end up losing your husband, because he will sense your disappointment in him. Your low opinion of him will inevitably leak out in disparaging comments and wound him deeply. He will withdraw emotionally and maybe even physically.[4]

Not surprisingly, the more I stopped offering my opinions and direction, the more John stepped up to the plate. He began by praying with me before he left for work. Make no mistake: *For years I resisted the urge to join in.* Instead, I just basked in the knowledge that John was doing this for me.

Finally, I did ask to participate. I started by adding a short prayer after John's. Later, during one of our challenging seasons, John requested that we read Scripture together in the mornings. *Yes!* It's what I had always wanted. And it's something I now look forward to every day.

Of course, many couples aren't on the same page spiritually and are truly unequally yoked. When this is the case, it's even more important to recognize that your words and actions will either draw your spouse toward faith or push him away. You also need to realize that it isn't up to you to save your spouse.

In the end, the issue of salvation is strictly between your spouse and God. It's the Holy Spirit's role to convict him of sin (John 16:8–11); only the Father can draw someone to Christ (John 6:44). God won't strong-arm your partner into following him; instead, God will honor his spiritual choices. As for you, the Bible gives Christian wives and husbands this responsibility: *love your spouse.* Love him or her unconditionally. Love him or her regardless of whether he or she ever bends the knee to Christ. Be devoted, be prayerful, be encouraging—but don't try to be responsible! You're not. Your spouse is. *Period.*

If you have been plagued by pangs of guilt due to feeling responsible for your husband's ongoing disinterest in God or church, you need to release yourself from that sentence. Yes, live out your faith as authentically as you can. Yes, confess to

God those personal failures and flaws that don't reflect well on Christ. Yes, apologize to your spouse when you haven't behaved in a Christ-like way. Yes, cooperate with the Holy Spirit as he works his transformational power in your life.

But, no, *don't* assume responsibility for what you cannot control. Don't wallow in blame for what ultimately is someone else's decision. Don't weigh yourself down with a burden that God never intended you to carry.[5]

And if your spouse is a God-seeker, the same mandate is true: It's up to *him* to grow closer to God. After all, no one ever reached God's throne by being pushed there. Oswald Chambers wrote, "It is easier to be an excessive fanatic than it is to be consistently faithful, because God causes an amazing humbling of our religious conceit when we are faithful to Him."[6]

Faithfulness can be achieved in the following ways:

1. **Focus on simplicity.** Don't try to model your devotional life after a Sunday school class or church service. Instead, look for simple devotional books at a Christian bookstore or online. One spouse can read the Scripture, and the other can read the devotion for the day. Even five minutes together is a great place to start. And once the habit is developed, you can experiment with making it more involved.

2. **Apply what you learn to life.** After spending time in God's Word, practice what you discover. There is no shortcut to holiness. Instead, during your evening conversations, talk about how God's Word applied to your day (see James 1:22–24).

3. **Connect with God.** There were times in the past when I focused more on learning *about* God than connecting *with* Him. That would be like John going on a date with me and spending the entire time with his nose in a book, researching the history of writers, or brunettes, or maybe the meaning of the name *Tricia*. Not that those things are bad in and of themselves, but it would be counterintuitive to enjoying the company of the living, breathing person beside him.

Sometimes we treat God the same way. We get so consumed with the facts *about* God that we forget He's real and desires an intimate relationship with us.

The cool thing is that as we mature and connect with the living God, the bigger He becomes to us. This idea is illustrated well in a snippet from C. S. Lewis's book *Prince Caspian*:

"Welcome, child," he said.

"Aslan," said Lucy, "you're bigger."

"That is because you are older, little one," answered he.

"Not because you are?"

"I am not. But every year you grow, you will find me bigger."[7]

That's what I want for me and John—to find God bigger as we grow together.

MY TAKE ON IT

God holds the whole world in the palm of His hand, and without Him nothing would stay together. (That's my own paraphrase of Colossians 1:17: "He is before all things, and in Him all things hold together.") Can you imagine the entire world just exploding? That's what I think of when I read that verse. And I imagine God's hand holding everything together and in position. That's a very comforting thought to me—and it really helps when I feel like life has me in over my head. I *know* that God is in control. He knows me. He knows what's going on. And nothing is happening that He is not aware of. I also know that God loves me—personally—and that I can trust Him in every situation. Sometimes it's easy to forget that and lose focus. But trusting in God's presence, power, and promises really helps me take that deep breath and keep moving forward.

—MD, born in 1968

New Jersey, married eleven years

I just keep remembering that in order to give of myself to my family, I must fill myself up with God first. If I don't connect with Him, my day is so much harder and I am not the wife or mother that I really want to be. Things tick me off quicker, my patience is thinner, and my tongue is much sharper. But if I just give myself time to ask God what His plans are and then *listen*, I seem to stress less and smile more!

—Kristy, born in 1971

Texas, married fifteen years

If you have an unsaved spouse, pray! That's what I did for Dan. And that's what Stephen Baldwin's wife did for him—she spent an hour every morning and every night on her face in the bedroom. I would love to meet her.

—Angela, born in 1977

Idaho, married seven years

Straight from the Heart

You say it's easy, but who's to say?
BRYAN ADAMS, *CUTS LIKE A KNIFE, 1983,* A&M

One of the most powerful things a couple can spend time doing together is praying.

"Would you like to divorce-proof your marriage? Then make time every day to pray with your spouse," writes Dr. Greg Smalley in *The Marriage You've Always Dreamed Of.* "When you both come before a holy and loving God in a posture of trust and dependence, you invite him to accomplish in your marriage what only he can do....They also see each other regularly humbling themselves before God....Couples who pray together every day have a divorce rate that is less than 1 percent." [8]

Prayer in marriage should be less about pleading our case before God and more about asking Him to change our hearts. James 1:5–8 says,

> If you need wisdom—if you want to know what God wants you to do—ask him, and he will gladly tell you. He will not resent your asking. But when you ask him, be sure that you really expect him to answer, for a doubtful mind is as unsettled as a wave of the sea that is driven and tossed by the wind. People like that should not expect to receive anything from the Lord. They can't make up their minds. They waver back and forth in everything they do. (NLT)

If you're like me, you love the idea of praying, of bringing your requests before God; however sometimes it is intimidating to pray with your spouse—you don't know what to say.

The best thing is to take small steps. Don't feel as if you have to start off with a twenty-point prayer list covering every aspect of your lives. Instead, address one or two of the most pressing issues in your lives, and then take them before God together. Realize that He has a perfect plan for these situations, and open your hearts to Him.

Also, remember that if you struggle with shared prayer, it may be because you have a true enemy, Satan. Satan knows the power of a husband and wife praying together, and he wants to disrupt it. He loves to take advantage of our embarrassment and vulnerability! He'll do whatever he can to stop you and your spouse from enjoying something that God really wants for you.

One of my favorite illustrations of married prayer is one my mother-in-law shared with me years ago. Early in my marriage to John, she told me that our marital relationship is like a triangle: At the base points of the triangle are John and me, and at the pinnacle is Jesus. As we both draw closer to Jesus, we'll find ourselves drawing closer to one another as well.

I love that!

My prayer for you is that from this day out, you will move closer to God and closer to each other. There could be nothing better!

MY TAKE ON IT

Marriage is another tool God uses to change us as individuals. Marriage pushes me to my knees. It reminds me how much I need God's grace and forgiveness. And it reminds me how completely human I am. In the process, like iron sharpening iron, I am made each day more into the image of the woman God placed me on earth to be.

—Cara, born in 1974

Indiana, married ten years

Prayer has made my marriage what it's supposed to be. Prayer changed my husband's heart, and it changed mine in how I see my husband.

—Allison, born in 1974

Florida, married thirteen years

God treasures me. He desires me. His hand rests upon me. His touch is gentle. His breath is sweet. His heart is pure. He longs for me and pursues me without end. This is what romance should look like. It is what we must work toward in our marriage.

—Michelle, born in 1971

Ohio, married thirteen years

Good-Bye

Never close, never far, always there when I needed a friend...

NIGHT RANGER, SEVEN WISHES, 1985, MCA RECORDS

I'm going to end this book with one final prayer—not only for you and your family, but for all Gen X couples. God has called *us* to be a part of this time in history. And, two by two, we can make a difference.

If you feel led, copy this prayer and pray it daily. Pray that God will unify us and unite our hearts and vision for this generation of couples. Trust that He will be faithful to do so.

> *I pray for you constantly, asking God, the glorious Father of our Lord Jesus Christ, to give you **spiritual wisdom** and **understanding**, so that you might **grow in your knowledge of God**. I pray that your **hearts will be flooded with light** so that you can **understand the wonderful future** he has promised to those he called. I want you to **realize what a rich and glorious inheritance** he has given to his people.*
>
> *I pray that you will **begin to understand the incredible greatness of his power** for us who believe him. This is the same mighty power that raised Christ from the dead and seated him in the place of honor at God's right hand in the heavenly realm. Now he is far above any ruler or authority or power or leader or anything else in this world or in the world to come. (Ephesians 1:16–21, NLT, emphasis added)*

Imagine—the same power that raised Christ from the dead is available to you and your spouse. May you continue to grasp, day by day, how truly amazing that concept is. And may Christ work in you in all these areas, as you seek Him…together.

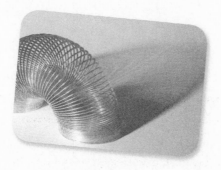

DIGGING DEEPER

Discussion Questions and Scripture References

INTRODUCTION: WHITE WEDDING

1. Do you think our generation views marriage differently than previous generations? Why or why not?

2. What do you think are some of the main struggles our generation deals with concerning marriage? Why do you think we experience these struggles?

3. Did you plan as diligently for your marriage as for your wedding? Why or why not?

4. What hopes do you have for our generation concerning marriage?

ϵ ϵ ϵ

1 YOU MIGHT THINK: DEALING WITH UNREALISTIC EXPECTATIONS IN THE REALITY OF MARRIAGE

1. It is not uncommon after you marry to look at your spouse and wonder, *Did I marry the right person?* This question tends to focus on your spouse's negative traits. How can you overcome this way of thinking?

2. Was there a time when you experienced a reality check? What were some of your expectations of your spouse when you first got married?

3. Read Genesis 3:16; Mark 10:6–9; 1 Corinthians 7:2–16; Ephesians 5:22–32. According to God, what are some "expectations" from marriage?

4. How have your expectations of your spouse changed over the years?

5. What does the Bible say about honoring and respecting your spouse?

6. Do you think Gen Xers have different expectations than their parents/ grandparents did? What are they? How should Gen Xers handle them?

Digging Deeper

Genesis 3:16

Mark 10:6–9

1 Corinthians 7:2–16

Ephesians 5:22–32

❝ ❝ ❝

2 HISTORY NEVER REPEATS: REVISITING YOUR RELATIONSHIP ROLE MODELS

1. What is your history? Make a brief list, cataloging the events in your life from birth onward. Note where you came from and where God has taken you. What themes has God worked in your life?

2. If you could go back in time and offer yourself advice about dating and marriage, what would it be?

3. How is your marriage different from your parents' marriage? Did you make a conscious effort to ensure that there would be differences? Similarities? What patterns (healthy or not) from your parents' marriage do you see in your own marriage?

4. Think about the cultural and generational influences that affected you growing up. How have they carried over into your marriage? In what ways has God enabled you to overcome problematic influences?

5. Think about your marriage. What are you teaching your children about marriage through your words and actions? Are you conveying the message you want to? If not, what should you work to change?

Digging Deeper

 2 Corinthians 12:9–10

 Malachi 2:13–16

 Matthew 9:3–9

 Romans 5:1–6

ε ε ε

3 TOGETHER FOREVER: COMMITTED FOR LIFE

1. What are your goals for your marriage? How are these different from your parents' goals for their marriage?
2. In what ways have you committed to making your marriage last?
3. What steps have you taken to affirm this commitment?
4. Have you ever faced a time in your marriage when you thought it would be easier to give up than work through problems?
5. What is your biggest struggle when it comes to lifelong commitment?

Digging Deeper

 Ephesians 5:23

 Mark 10:9

 Romans 12:9–10

 1 Peter 3:7

ε ε ε

4 UNDER PRESSURE: FINDING BALANCE

1. Consider your marriage and family life. Are you doing a good job balancing hectic schedules, family time, and couple time? Why or why not?
2. What in your life seems to take priority? Are there any priorities that need to be changed?
3. In what ways have you succeeded in putting your spouse first in your marriage?

4. Think about the last date you had with your spouse. What did you do, and what did you talk about? Looking ahead to your next date, what would you like to change about your time together?

5. Are you controlled more by your own expectations of yourself or the expectations of others? What is God saying to you about this?

Digging Deeper

Mark 8:38

Luke 10:38–42

Exodus 20:8–11

Psalm 127:2

€ € €

5 I REMEMBER YOU: OVERCOMING THE BOND OF PAST RELATIONSHIPS

1. In what ways have your own past relationships hurt your marriage?

2. In what ways have your spouse's past relationships hurt your marriage?

3. How have you and your spouse overcome past relationships? What problems do you still need to overcome?

4. How do you and your spouse hold each other accountable? Do you find this important in marriage?

5. How do you handle temptations outside your marriage?

Digging Deeper

Psalm 139:23–24

2 Peter 2:9

1 Corinthians 10:13

Luke 17:1–4

Galatians 6:7–8

€ € €

6 IN YOUR EYES: INTIMACY

1. How do you define intimacy? How does your spouse define intimacy? Are your definitions different?

2. Do you struggle with opening up to others? If so, do you think it harms or puts a strain on your relationships? Why?

3. Do you hide your sinfulness from your spouse? What are you hoping to accomplish by doing that? Why do you think God tells us to confess our sins to one another?

4. What can you do to make yourself more transparent? Is being transparent important?

5. What role does fear play, if any, in the way you handle your relationships?

Digging Deeper

Matthew 11:28–30

Proverbs 5:8

Romans 3:23

Ecclesiastes 4:9–12

James 5:16

7 AGAINST ALL ODDS: MEDIA MATTERS

1. How does the media affect your marriage?

2. Do you and your husband agree on media choices?

3. How do you handle your differences?

4. Considering how inundated we are by the media, how do you keep from letting too much of the world and worldly thinking into your life?

5. How did your media exposure as a child shape who you became as an adult? What ideas about yourself and the culture around you did you adopt as your own? Has that led to any problems or difficulties as you matured and got married?

Digging Deeper

Psalm 101:3

Romans 12:2

1 Corinthians 15:33

Philippians 4:8

1 John 2:15–17

Ephesians 5:15–17

8 SWEET CHILD O' MINE: CHILDREN REDEFINE "MARRIAGE PARTNERSHIP"

1. In what ways have children changed your marriage? What specific challenges has raising children brought to your marriage?

2. In what ways has child rearing made your marriage stronger?

3. How do your expectations of what a Christian mother/father should look like compare to reality? What conflicts does that create?

4. In what ways do your parenting styles differ, and how do you handle those differences?

5. A friend once told me that the only thing I get to take to heaven with me when I die is my children. How might this mind-set define your goals as a parenting team?

Digging Deeper

Psalm 25:4–5

Ephesians 6:4

Galatians 5:22–24

Philippians 4:4–7

1 Peter 3:7

9 DIRTY LAUNDRY: EVERYDAY STUFF OF LIFE

1. In what ways does God's Word define roles and responsibilities in your marriage?

2. Do you find it hard to serve your spouse when the work seems overwhelming and you're worn out?

3. How do gender roles define the breakdown of responsibilities in your home?

4. How have our views of roles and responsibilities changed from those generations before us?

5. The roles of man and woman are defined by God as different but equal. Are any of the conflicts in your marriage caused by rebellion to God's design?

Digging Deeper

Proverbs 31:10–31

Matthew 25:34–46

Romans 12:10

1 Corinthians 11:3

1 Corinthians 11:7–9

e e e

10 HANDS TO HEAVEN: CHURCH SERVICE

1. How important do you believe it is for you and your husband to serve in your church?

2. Do you believe that God has placed you in His church, for His purpose? Why or why not?

3. In your opinion, what is the purpose of the church—to meet your needs or to meet the needs of others?

4. Has serving in the church, or in ministry, ever placed a strain on your marriage and/or family life?

5. What is the God-ordained order for your family? Is this true of every family?

6. What does worship have to do with service and obedience?

Digging Deeper

Matthew 22:37–40

John 12:34–35

Romans 12:1

Galatians 5:13–15

Ephesians 4:11–16

❝ ❝ ❝

11 LET MY LOVE OPEN THE DOOR: ROMANCING YOUR SPOUSE

1. How does true romance differ from what we see in the movies?

2. In what ways does your spouse romance you, and vice versa? What hinders romance in your marriage?

3. How does God's example of love and romance influence and guide your relationship?

4. By your example, what are you teaching your children about love and romance? How is this different from what you learned as a child?

Digging Deeper

Genesis 2:18–25

Song of Songs 8:6–7

Jeremiah 31:3

Ecclesiastes 9:9

1 John 3:18

❝ ❝ ❝

12 IF YOU DON'T KNOW ME BY NOW: DIFFERENT BY DESIGN

1. What is the role of a wife as defined in the Bible?

2. What is the role of a husband as defined in the Bible?

3. Evaluate the role you play in your marriage. Does it follow God's standard?
4. What does biblical submission look like? What does submission look like in your marriage?
5. In what ways do your differences as man/woman benefit your marriage?
6. When is your partnership most successful?

Digging Deeper

Philippians 3:12–21

Colossians 3:18–19

1 Peter 2:2–7

1 Peter 2:8–9

ℰ ℰ ℰ

13 LOVE IS A BATTLEFIELD: CONFLICT RESOLUTION FOR COUPLES

1. What are the top three things that cause conflict in your marriage?
2. In marriage, we need to be other-centered rather than self-centered. Would you say that in your marriage you work toward this ideal?
3. Do you pursue peace or seek your own way? What role does anger, blame, or bitterness play in your conflicts?
4. Would you say your conflict tactics are healthy and aid to better your marriage?
5. What do you do well? What areas need work?
6. Do you struggle with backing down for the sake of ending the conflict?

Digging Deeper

Proverbs 25:21–24

James 1:19–25

James 4:1–3, 6-7, 11

Ephesians 4:26–27, 29–5:2

1 Peter 3:7–8

ℰ ℰ ℰ

14 BE GOOD TO YOURSELF: TAKING CARE OF YOU

1. What do you do to take care of yourself?

2. How do you care for yourself without becoming obsessed or losing sight of your priorities? When does care for self go too far?

3. Do you think it's important to be visually appealing for your spouse?

4. How do you take care of yourself spiritually?

5. If you or your spouse is "letting things slide," what words might be encouraging without coming across as judgmental and/or hurtful?

6. What does the Bible say about taking care of ourselves?

Digging Deeper

Proverbs 3:6–8

Ephesians 6:10–19

1 Thessalonians 5:11, 14, 19

2 Thessalonians 3:5

1 Peter 2:2

❮ ❮ ❮

15 IS THERE SOMETHING I SHOULD KNOW? COMMUNICATION

1. How does your self-talk affect your relationship?

2. How does body language affect your communication? What roles do tone of voice and facial expression play in communicating effectively?

3. What are some of your communication struggles?

4. What communication strategies have benefited your marriage? Which ones do you need to stop using?

5. How do you take time to listen to all voices in your life—e.g., your husband, parents, children, neighbors, friends, employer, co-workers, etc.? Are there any that you need to get rid of?

Digging Deeper

Proverbs 10:19

Proverbs 12:18–19

Proverbs 15:28

James 1:19

James 3:5–12

❝ ❝ ❝

16 DANCING IN THE SHEETS: LOVEMAKING

1. How is sex as portrayed in the media different from reality? What can you do if your sex life doesn't meet your expectations?

2. Is sex in your marriage used as a way to avoid problems or to bring you closer? Should you ever use sex to get what you want?

3. The Song of Songs is a very sensual book. Why do you think God put it in the Bible?

4. How do you find the time to keep things passionate between you and your spouse in the midst of busy schedules and children?

5. Do you think sex is as important to men as communication is to women? How is this true in your marriage?

Digging Deeper

Song of Songs

1 Corinthians 7:2–5

❝ ❝ ❝

17 MAKE IT REAL: DREAMS AND GOALS

1. How have your dreams and goals changed since you married? Have you and your spouse's goals remained separate, or have they merged?

2. What role does God's will play in your dreams and goals? Do your dreams and goals include fulfilling God's purpose for your life?

3. How has your spouse helped you achieve your dreams?
4. Do you agree or disagree that God gives us the desires of our hearts, enables us to fulfill them, and uses them to serve His purpose? How has that been true in your life?
5. Have you ever followed a dream/goal you thought was from God but then realized wasn't? How did that affect you, your faith, your family, and your marriage?

Digging Deeper
> Psalm 63:8
> Ecclesiastes 2:11
> Micah 6:6–8
> 1 Corinthians 13:12
> 1 Corinthians 15:10

18 EVERYTHING I OWN: MONEY MATTERS

1. In your marriage, do you control the money or does it control you?
2. Are finances a source of conflict between you and your spouse?
3. It is difficult to be content in our "want it all, want it now" world. How do you and your spouse resist this mentality? What do you do to protect yourself from worldly desires?
4. How do you and your spouse deal with the *B* word (budget)? As your children watch you deal with finances, what are they learning?
5. If you don't have a lot of money, how can you be content with what God has given you?
6. If you are wealthy, how do you keep yourself pure and holy?

Digging Deeper
> Ecclesiastes 5:10
> Matthew 6:24

Acts 8:20–22

1 Timothy 6:10

Hebrews 13:5

❝ ❝ ❝

19 HIGHER LOVE: GROWING IN GOD

1. Think about this statement: *Marriage is intended to make you holy, not happy.* Do you agree with it? Why or why not?

2. What sort of impact does spending time alone with God have on your ability to be a loving and service-minded spouse?

3. What do you do if you and your spouse have different spiritual beliefs and/or disagree about which church to attend?

4. If your spouse is an unbeliever, do your actions point him toward God?

5. Have you ever run ahead of God and done it your own way? What was the result?

6. What have you learned about God by bringing your problems to Him and letting Him work out the solutions?

7. Has prayer changed your marriage? If so, how might you share that with others?

Digging Deeper

Psalm 143:10

Proverbs 27:17

Matthew 26:41

2 Corinthians 3:17–18

Colossians 4:2

Acknowledgments

John, seventeen years and better each one. I love you.

Cory, Leslie, and Nathan. Thanks for being loving and understanding kids.

My loving family...Grandma, Mom, Dad, Ronnie, John, and Darlyne. Your prayers hold me up!

Stacey, Lesley, and Melissa—great sisters to talk about marriage with.

Amy Lathrop, my everything friend and everything girl. Thanks!

My agent, Janet Kobobel Grant. An awesome mentor and guide.

The Multnomah team...thank you! Special thanks to my editors, David Kopp and Steffany Woolsey.

My unofficial editors: Cara Putman, Amy Lathrop, Lesley Lafuze, and Katie Schnee. You're the best!

Finally, this book wouldn't have been written if not for the *amazing* Gen Xers who gave their input and answered all my many, many questions:

Carolyn Barndt	Rene Gutteridge
Scott Barndt	Jeanette Hanscome
Sherry Boles	Norman Hanscome
Heidi Burns	Jay Hatfield
Cammie Carman	Kristi Hatfield
Koryn Chatriand	Andora Henson
Stephanie Clancy	Jessica Holst
Christopher Colter	Kevin Holst
Tiffany Colter	J. W. Hortenberry Jr.
Michelle Dickson	Michelle Hortenberry
Robert Dickson	Janet Kawash
Dena Dyer	Lesley LaFuze
Caren Fullerton	Amy Lathrop

Mona Marushak

Angela Meuser

Dani Meyers

Stacey Moyer

Amy Parker

Cara Putman

Pattie Reitz

Melissa Renner

Jenn Riale

Dana Tappen Rivera

Dee Rockman

Jennifer Rudnick

Katie Schnee

Janelle Schneider

Jeff Sumpolec

Sarah Anne Sumpolec

Amy Wallace

Allison Wilson

Chris Wilson

Notes

Introduction

1. Neil Clark Warren, *The Triumphant Marriage* (Colorado Springs, CO: Focus on the Family, 1995), 6.
2. Graeme Codrington and Sue Grant-Marshall, *Mind the Gap!* (London: Penguin, 2005), 1.
3. Patrick and Connie Lawrence, *How to Build a More Intimate Marriage* (Nashville, TN: Thomas Nelson, 1993), 5.
4. "Generation X," wikipedia.com. http://en.wikipedia.org/wiki/Generation_X (accessed 7 June 2007).
5. Center for Demography and Ecology at the University of Wisconsin-Madison, US Bureau of Labor Statistics, US Census Bureau.
6. Stanley Kurtz, "Marriage and the Gen Xer," *Hoover Digest* 2002, no. 4, www.hoover.org/publications/digest/4495926.html (accessed 7 June 2007).
7. Cliff Zukin, "A Closer Look at Generation X," News in the Next Century On-Line Resources, www.rtnda.org/resources/genx/genlook2.htm (accessed 7 June 2007).
8. Patrick F. Fagan et al., "The Positive Effects of Marriage: A Book of Charts," The Heritage Foundation, www.heritage.org/Research/Features/Marriage/index.cfm (accessed 7 June 2007).
9. Patrick F. Fagan, Robert E. Rector, and Lauren R. Noyes, "Why Congress Should Ignore Radical Feminist Opposition to Marriage," The Heritage Foundation, www.heritage.org/Research/Family/bg1662.cfm (accessed 7 June 2007).
10. Fagan et al., "The Positive Effects of Marriage."
11. Patricia Wen, "Gen X Dad," *Boston Globe*, 16 January 2005, www.boston.com/news/globe/magazine/articles/2005/01/16/gen_x_dad/ (accessed 7 June 2007).
12. David Athens, "Gen X hits big 4-0," *Post-Trib.com*, www.iun.edu/~newsnw/articles/07-19-05_post_trib.pdf (accessed 7 June 2007).

Chapter 1

1. Willard F. Harley Jr., *His Needs, Her Needs* (Grand Rapids, MI: Fleming H. Revell, 2004), 82.
2. Author unknown.
3. Mike Mason, *The Mystery of Marriage* (Sisters, OR: Multnomah, 1985), 100.
4. Beth Moore, *Breaking Free* (Nashville, TN: Liberty, 1999), 194, quoted in Sharon Jaynes, *Dreams of a Woman* (Wheaton, IL: Tyndale House, 2004), 3.
5. Cindi Wood, *The Frazzled Female* (Nashville, TN: Lifeway, 2004), 52.
6. *Life Application Bible Commentary: John* (Wheaton, IL: Tyndale House, 1993), 215.
7. Mason, *The Mystery of Marriage*, 93.

Chapter 2

1. Graeme Codrington and Sue Grant-Marshall, *Mind the Gap!* (London: Penguin, 2005), 49.
2. Jen Abbas, *Generation Ex* (Colorado Springs, CO: WaterBrook, 2004), 2.

3. Pamela Paul, *The Starter Marriage and the Future of Matrimony* (New York: Villard Books, 2002), 15.

4. Dr. Rick and Kathy Hicks, *Boomers, Xers, and Other Strangers* (Wheaton, IL: Tyndale House, 1999), 13.

5. Judith S. Wallerstein, Julia M. Lewis, and Sandra Blakeslee, *The Unexpected Legacy of Divorce* (New York: Hyperion, 2000), xiii.

6. Paul, *Starter Marriage*, 35.

7. The Barna Group, "America's Faith Is Changing, but Beneath the Surface," 18, March 2003, www.barna.org/FlexPage.aspx?Page=BarnaUpdate&BarnaUpdateID=135 (accessed 13 December 2006).

8. Abbas, *Generation Ex*, 21.

9. Roper Reports 1998, as quoted in Pamela Paul, *Starter Marriage*, x.

10. Paul, *Starter Marriage*, xiii.

Chapter 3

1. Jim Burns, *Creating an Intimate Marriage* (Bloomington, MN: Bethany House, 2006), 51.

2. Pamela Paul, *The Starter Marriage and the Future of Matrimony* (New York: Villard Books, 2002), 16.

3. Pam Kelley, "Can This Marriage Be Saved?" *Charlotte Observer*, 11 February 2001, as quoted in Sharon Jaynes, *Becoming the Woman of His Dreams* (Eugene, OR: Harvest House, 2005), 199.

4. Shaunti Feldhahn, *For Women Only* (Sisters, OR: Multnomah, 2004), 22.

5. Dr. Emerson Eggerichs, *Love and Respect* (Brentwood, TN: Integrity, 2004), 113.

6. Caroline Overington, "Gen X Keen on the ABCs of Raising Gen Y," *The Age Online*, 24 July 2004, www.reachadvisors.com/agearticle.html (accessed 4 May 2006).

7. Myron A. Marty, *Daily Life in the United States 1960–1990* (Westport, CT: Greenwood, 1997), 185.

Chapter 4

1. Graeme Codrington and Sue Grant-Marshall, *Mind the Gap!* (London: Penguin, 2005), 75.

2. Codrington and Grant-Marshall, *Mind the Gap!*, 20.

3. Jeffrey Kluger, "Why We Worry About the Things We Shouldn't…and Ignore the Things We Should," *Time*, 4 December 2006, 66.

4. Leslie Vernick, *How to Act Right When Your Spouse Acts Wrong* (Colorado Springs, CO: WaterBrook, 2001), 112–13.

5. Dennis and Barbara Rainey, *Staying Close* (Nashville, TN: Thomas Nelson, 2003), 97.

6. Dave Stoop, *Self-Talk: Key to Personal Growth* (Old Tappan, NJ: Fleming H. Revell, 1982), 12.

7. Rainey, *Staying Close*, 96.

8. Willard F. Harley Jr., *His Needs, Her Needs* (Grand Rapids, MI: Fleming H. Revell, 2001), 134–35.

9. Mike Mason, *The Mystery of Marriage* (Sisters, OR: Multnomah, 1985), 122–23.

10. Pamela Paul, *The Starter Marriage and the Future of Matrimony* (New York: Villard Books, 2002), xii.

Chapter 5

1. Linda Dillow and Lorraine Pintus, *Intimate Issues* (Colorado Springs, CO: WaterBrook, 1999), 86.

2. Toni S. Poynter, *Now and Forever* (Chicago, IL: Loyola, 2004), 99.

Chapter 6

1. Dr. Rick and Kathy Hicks, *Boomers, Xers, and Other Strangers* (Wheaton, IL: Tyndale House, 1999), 37–38.
2. Judith S. Wallerstein, Julia M. Lewis, and Sandra Blakeslee, *The Unexpected Legacy of Divorce* (New York: Hyperion, 2000), xxxv.
3. Jen Abbas, *Generation Ex* (Colorado Springs, CO: WaterBrook, 2004), 183.
4. Mike Mason, *The Mystery of Marriage* (Sisters, OR: Multnomah, 1985), 22.
5. Sharon Jaynes, *Becoming the Woman of His Dreams* (Eugene, OR: Harvest House, 2005), 128–29.
6. Mason, *Mystery of Marriage*, 102.
7. Dennis and Barbara Rainey, *Staying Close* (Nashville, TN: Thomas Nelson, 2003), 3.
8. Hicks, *Boomers, Xers, and Other Strangers*, 293.
9. Lois and Alan Gordon, *The Columbia Chronicles of American Life 1910–1992* (New York: Columbia University Press, 1995), 672, as quoted in Hicks, *Boomers, Xers, and Other Strangers*, 179.
10. Victor Bondi, ed., *American Decades 1980–1989* (Detroit: Gale Research, 1996).

Chapter 7

1. Dr. Rick and Kathy Hicks, *Boomers, Xers, and Other Strangers* (Wheaton, IL: Tyndale House, 1999), 185.
2. Sheri and Bob Stritof, "Kick the Television Out of Your Bedroom!" about.com, http://marriage.about.com/b/a/235983.htm (accessed 7 June 2007).
3. Ann Oldenburg, "The Divine Miss Winfrey?" *USA Today*, 11 May 2006, D1-2, http://www.preachingtoday.com/36682 (accessed June 7, 2007).
4. Oswald Chambers, *My Utmost for His Highest* (1935; repr., Grand Rapids, MI: Discovery House, 1992), September 15 entry.

Chapter 8

1. Dennis and Barbara Rainey, *Staying Close* (Nashville, TN: Thomas Nelson, 2003), 115.
2. Gary Chapman, *The Four Seasons of Marriage* (Wheaton, IL: Tyndale House, 2005), 4.
3. Dr. Rick and Kathy Hicks, *Boomers, Xers, and Other Strangers* (Wheaton, IL: Tyndale House, 1999), 293.
4. Dr. John Roseman, "Promise Keepers Challenges Husbands, but What About Wives"? as quoted in Sharon Jaynes, *Becoming the Woman of His Dreams* (Eugene, OR: Harvest House, 2005), 164–65.
5. George Barna, *Baby Busters* (Chicago: Northfield, 1994), 34–38.

Chapter 9

1. Oswald Chambers, *My Utmost for His Highest* (Grand Rapids, MI: Discovery House), November 14 entry.
2. Robert Lewis and William Hendricks, *Rocking the Roles* (Colorado Springs, CO: NavPress, 1998), 41.
3. Arlie Hochschild, *The Second Shift: Working Parents and the Revolution at Home* (New York: Viking Penguin, 1989), 3–4.
4. Mike Mason, *The Mystery of Marriage* (Sisters, OR: Multnomah, 1985), 123.
5. Toni S. Poynter, *Now and Forever* (Chicago, IL: Loyola, 2004), quoted in Greg Smalley, *The Marriage You've Always Dreamed Of* (Wheaton, IL: Tyndale House, 2005), 40.

6. Deniece Schofield, *Confessions of a Happily Organized Family* (Cincinnati, OH: Betterway Books, 1997), 9.

7. Schofield, *Happily Organized Family*, 60.

8. Gary Thomas, *Sacred Marriage* (Grand Rapids, MI: Zondervan, 2000), 32.

9. Dr. Craig Glickman, *Solomon's Song of Love* (West Monroe, LA: Howard, 2004), 143–44.

Chapter 10

1. Dr. Rick and Kathy Hicks, *Boomers, Xers, and Other Strangers* (Wheaton, IL: Tyndale House, 1999), 185.

2. The Barna Group, "America's Faith Is Changing," 18 March 2003, www.barna.org/FlexPage.aspx?Page=BarnaUpdate&BarnaUpdateID=135 (accessed 7 June 2007).

3. Hicks, *Boomers, Xers, and Other Strangers*, 186.

4. Hicks, *Boomers, Xers, and Other Strangers*, 264.

5. Jen Abbas, *Generation Ex* (Colorado Springs, CO: WaterBrook, 2004), 163.

6. Abbas, *Generation Ex*, 162–63.

7. The Barna Group, "Born-Again Christians Just as Likely to Divorce as Are Non-Christians," 8 September 2004, www.barna.org/FlexPage.aspx?Page=BarnaUpdate&BarnaUpdateID=170 (accessed 7 June 2007).

8. Graeme Codrington and Sue Grant-Marshall, *Mind the Gap!* (London: Penguin, 2005), 253.

9. Codrington and Grant-Marshall, *Mind the Gap!*, 233.

Chapter 11

1. Myron A. Marty, *Daily Life in the United States 1960–1990* (Westport, CT: Greenwood, 1997), 230.

2. Romance Writers of America, Reader Statistics, www.rwanational.org/eweb/dynamicpage.aspx?webcode=StatisticsReader (accessed 4 January 2007).

3. Toni S. Poynter, *Now and Forever* (Chicago, IL: Loyola, 2004), 122.

4. Poynter, *Now and Forever*, 87.

5. Ed Wheat, *Love Life for Every Married Couple*, as quoted in William and Nancie Carmichael, *601 Quotes About Marriage and Family* (Wheaton, IL: Tyndale House Publishers, 1998), 46.

6. Gary Chapman, *The Four Seasons of Marriage* (Wheaton, IL: Tyndale House, 2005), 154–55.

7. Dan B. Allender and Tremper Longman, *Intimate Allies*, as quoted in Carmichael, *Marriage and Family*, 37.

8. Poynter, *Now and Forever*, 132.

9. H. Norman Wright and Gary J. Oliver, *How to Change Your Spouse (Without Ruining Your Marriage)*, as quoted in Carmichael, *Marriage and Family*, 56.

10. Lynne C. Lancaster and David Stillman, *When Generations Collide* (New York: HarperCollins, 2003), 255.

Chapter 12

1. Toni S. Poynter, *Now and Forever* (Chicago, IL: Loyola, 2004), 36.

2. Pamela Paul, *The Starter Marriage and the Future of Matrimony* (New York: Villard Books, 2002), 38.

3. Gary Chapman, *The Four Seasons of Marriage* (Wheaton, IL: Tyndale House, 2005), 136.

4. Dr. Emerson Eggerichs, *Love and Respect* (Brentwood, TN: Integrity, 2004), 206–7.

5. Eggerichs, *Love and Respect*, 221.

6. Pamela Paul, *The Starter Marriage and the Future of Matrimony* (New York: Villard Books, 2002), 153.

7. Sharon Jaynes, *Becoming the Woman of His Dreams* (Eugene, OR: Harvest House, 2005), 204.

8. Shaunti and Jeff Feldhahn, *For Men Only: A Straightforward Guide to the Inner Lives of Women* (Sisters, OR: Multnomah, 2006), 25–26.

9. Shaunti and Jeff Feldhahn, *For Men Only*, 46–47.

Chapter 13

1. Elizabeth Cody Newenhuyse, "Serving Time on the California Coast," *Marriage Partnership*, as quoted in William and Nancie Carmichael, *601 Quotes About Marriage and Family* (Wheaton, IL: Tyndale House, 1998), 80.

2. Dr. Greg Smalley, *The Marriage You've Always Dreamed Of* (Wheaton, IL: Tyndale House, 2005), 38.

3. Smalley, *Marriage You've Always Dreamed Of*, 42.

4. Gary Chapman, *The Four Seasons of Marriage* (Wheaton, IL: Tyndale House, 2005), 83.

5. Madeleine L'Engle, *The Door Interviews*, as quoted in Carmichael, *Marriage and Family*, 84.

6. Mike Mason, *The Mystery of Marriage* (Sisters, OR: Multnomah, 1985), 104.

7. Toni S. Poynter, *Now and Forever* (Chicago, IL: Loyola, 2004), 57.

8. Smalley, *Marriage You've Always Dreamed Of*, 162–63.

9. C. S. Lewis, *Mere Christianity* (Nashville, TN: Broadman and Holman, 1996), 104.

10. Dr. Joseph C. Dillow et al., *Intimacy Ignited* (Colorado Springs, CO: NavPress, 2004), 213.

11. Dennis and Barbara Rainey, *Staying Close* (Nashville, TN: Thomas Nelson, 2003), 253.

12. Jen Abbas, *Generation Ex* (Colorado Springs, CO: WaterBrook, 2004), 188.

13. Chapman, *Four Seasons of Marriage*, 174.

Chapter 14

1. Dr. Greg Smalley, *The Marriage You've Always Dreamed Of* (Wheaton, IL: Tyndale House, 2005), 142.

2. Toni S. Poynter, *Now and Forever* (Chicago, IL: Loyola, 2004), 124.

3. Poynter, *Now and Forever*, 11.

4. Shaunti Feldhahn, *For Women Only* (Sisters, OR: Multnomah, 2004), 161.

5. Feldhahn, *For Women Only*, 162–63.

6. Dr. Les Parrott and Dr. Neil Clark Warren, *Love the Life You Live* (Wheaton, IL: Tyndale House, 2003), 147.

7. Dennis and Barbara Rainey, *Staying Close* (Nashville, TN: Thomas Nelson, 2003), 40–44.

Chapter 15

1. "The Eighties Club: The Politics and Pop Culture of the 1980s," http://eightiesclub.tripod.com/id44.htm (accessed 7 June 2007).

2. Jen Abbas, *Generation Ex* (Colorado Springs, CO: WaterBrook, 2004), 60–61.

3. Abbas, *Generation Ex*, 20.

4. Hugh Prather, *Notes to Myself*, as quoted in William and Nancie Carmichael, *601 Quotes About Marriage and Family* (Wheaton, IL: Tyndale House, 1998), 71.

5. Toni S. Poynter, *Now and Forever* (Chicago, IL: Loyola, 2004), 134.

6. Ralph Waldo Emerson, *The Conduct of Life.* Accessed at www.answers.com/topic/the-conduct-of-life-behavior.

7. Poynter, *Now and Forever*, 48.

8. Mary Rose O'Reilly, "Deep Listening: An Experimental Friendship," *Weavings*, as quoted in Carmichael, *Marriage and Family*, 70.

9. www.esquareleadership.com/quotations.htm.

10. Gary Chapman, *The Four Seasons of Marriage* (Wheaton, IL: Tyndale House, 2005), 108.

Chapter 16

1. Linda Dillow and Lorraine Pintus, *Intimate Issues* (Colorado Springs, CO: WaterBrook, 1999), 10.

2. Richard Nadler, "Birds, Bees, and ABC's," *National Review* Online, 13 September 1999, www.findarticles.com/p/articles/mi_m1282/is_8_51/ai_55746953 (accessed 7 June 2007).

3. Dr. Kevin Leman, *Sheet Music* (Wheaton, IL: Tyndale House, 2003), 23.

4. Dillow and Pintus, *Intimate Issues*, 10.

5. Dillow and Pintus, *Intimate Issues*, 7.

6. Dillow and Pintus, *Intimate Issues*, 47.

7. Shaunti Feldhahn, *For Women Only* (Sisters, OR: Multnomah, 2004), 92–93.

8. Shaunti and Jeff Feldhahn, *For Men Only* (Sisters, OR: Multnomah, 2006), 126–35.

9. Shaunti and Jeff Feldhahn, *For Men Only*, 133.

10. Dr. Joseph C. Dillow et al., *Intimacy Ignited* (Colorado Springs, CO: NavPress, 2004), 29.

11. Bill and Pam Farrel, *Red-Hot Monogamy* (Eugene, OR: Harvest House, 2006), 9.

12. "You Told Us," *Redbook* (February 2001), 12, as quoted in Leman, *Sheet Music*, 184.

13. Dillow et al., *Intimacy Ignited*, 56.

Chapter 17

1. Gary Chapman, *The Four Seasons of Marriage* (Wheaton, IL: Tyndale House, 2005), 5.

2. Mike Mason, *The Mystery of Marriage* (Sisters, OR: Multnomah, 1985), 42.

3. Wesley L. Duewel, *Let God Guide You Daily* (Grand Rapids, MI: Zondervan, 1988), 182.

4. Dr. Greg Smalley, *The Marriage You've Always Dreamed Of* (Wheaton, IL: Tyndale House, 2005), 85.

5. Drs. Les and Leslie Parrott, "Skimming the Surface?" *Marriage Partnership*, as quoted in William and Nancie Carmichael, *601 Quotes About Marriage and Family* (Wheaton, IL: Tyndale House, 1998), 37.

6. Sharon Jaynes, *Dreams of a Woman* (Wheaton, IL: Tyndale House, 2004), 202–3.

7. Dr. Richard Carlson, *Don't Sweat the Small Stuff* (New York: Hyperion, 1997), 20.

8. Jaynes, *Dreams of a Woman*, 215.

9. Jaynes, *Dreams of a Woman*, 221.

10. Chapman, *Four Seasons of Marriage*, 4.

11. Graeme Codrington and Sue Grant-Marshall, *Mind the Gap!* (London: Penguin, 2005), 91.

Chapter 18

1. Dr. Rick and Kathy Hicks, *Boomers, Xers, and Other Strangers* (Wheaton, IL: Tyndale House, 1999), 254.
2. Victor Bondi, ed., *American Decades: 1980–1989* (Detroit: Gale Research, 1996), x.
3. Christopher Lasch, *Culture of Narcissism*, as quoted in Dennis and Barbara Rainey, *Staying Close* (Nashville, TN: Thomas Nelson, 2003), 59–60.
4. Sharon Jaynes, *Becoming the Woman of His Dreams* (Eugene, OR: Harvest House, 2005), 58.
5. Willard F. Harley Jr., *His Needs, Her Needs* (Grand Rapids, MI: Fleming H. Revell, 2001), 67–68.
6. "Christmas: The Growing Backlash Against Greed," *The Week*, 10 December 2004, as quoted in *Leadership Journal Online*, www.preachingtoday.com/26019 (accessed 7 June 2007).
7. Larry Burkett, *Great Is Thy Faithfulness* (Uhrichsville, OH: Promise), July 7 entry.

Chapter 19

1. Pamela Paul, *The Starter Marriage and the Future of Matrimony* (New York: Villard Books, 2002), 90.
2. Robert Lewis and William Hendricks, *Rocking the Roles* (Colorado Springs, CO: NavPress, 1998), 219.
3. Shaunti Feldhahn, *For Women Only* (Sisters, OR: Multnomah, 2004), 56.
4. Lee Strobel and Leslie Strobel, *Surviving a Spiritual Mismatch in Marriage* (Grand Rapids, MI: Zondervan, 2002), 68.
5. Strobel, *Surviving a Spiritual Mismatch*, 40.
6. Oswald Chambers, *My Utmost for His Highest* (Grand Rapids, MI: Discovery House), November 14 entry.
7. C. S. Lewis, *The Wisdom of Narnia* (New York: HarperCollins, 2001), 141.
8. Dr. Greg Smalley, *The Marriage You've Always Dreamed Of* (Wheaton, IL: Tyndale House, 2005), 194.